A House in the City

Isaac Braithwaite (1810–1890). Partner 1833.
Senior Partner 1855–1888

A House in the City

A Study of the City and of the Stock Exchange based on the Records of Foster & Braithwaite 1825–1975

W. J. READER

Research by Judy Slinn

B. T. BATSFORD LTD, LONDON

First published 1979
Reprinted 1980
Copyright W. J. Reader 1979
Printed in Great Britain by
Redwood Burn Limited
Trowbridge & Esher
for the Publishers
B. T. Batsford Ltd,
4 Fitzhardinge Street, London W1H 0AH
ISBN 0 7134 1647 5

Contents

List of Illustrations

Isaac Braithwaite *frontispiece*

Between pages 54 and 55

Between pages 118 and 119

Foreword

The history of the Stock Exchange has recently been surveyed by Professor E. Victor Morgan and W. A. Thomas and by Alan Jenkins. These authors had access to the archives of the Stock Exchange but not, I think, to the records of any individual firm. When, therefore, Mr David Braithwaite offered me the opportunity of writing a book on the history of the Stock Exchange based, so far as primary sources are concerned, on the records of a Stock Exchange firm—Foster & Braithwaite—I gladly accepted. This book is the result.

I have had unfailing help and encouragement, throughout a period of extreme difficulty for all firms on the Stock Exchange, from the present partners in Foster & Braithwaite, particularly Messrs David Braithwaite and Michael Savory, and from the staff of the firm generally. I am grateful also for much help, written and verbal, from Messrs J. N. and C. B. Savory and from Mr Arthur Braithwaite. Nobody has attempted to dictate what I have written and I should like to emphasise that no mistakes I have made nor opinions I express are to be attributed to anyone except myself.

I am greatly indebted to Mrs Slinn for her work on the primary sources, and to the staff of the Guildhall Library, London, where most of Foster & Braithwaite's archives are now lodged. I am grateful also to the authorities of

the Stock Exchange and of Lloyds Bank Limited for access
to manuscript records in their possession.

London   W. J. Reader.
September 1976

This book was commissioned to mark the one hundred
and fiftieth anniversary of the foundation of the firm. It
is late in appearing but we hope it may be accepted as a
serious contribution to the literature of the City.

    With this in mind we asked Dr Reader to paint the
picture as he saw it—'warts and all'—and we are grateful
to him for the friendly and painstaking way in which he
has carried out his task.

D.B.

JOHN DAVID CHRISTOPHER BRAITHWAITE

The present Partners wish to dedicate the publication of
this book to John David Christopher Braithwaite, following his death on 2 July 1978, for it had been his wish to
see the book published before his retirement as Senior
Partner.

London
February 1979

TABLE I—FOSTER

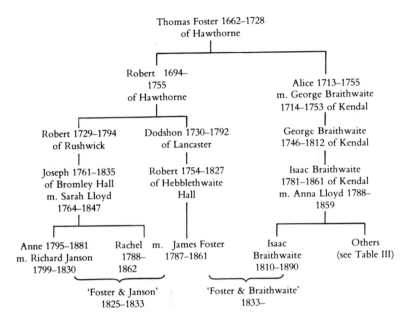

Thomas Foster 1662–1728
of Hawthorne

Robert 1694–1755
of Hawthorne

Alice 1713–1755
m. George Braithwaite
1714–1753 of Kendal

Robert 1729–1794
of Rushwick

Dodshon 1730–1792
of Lancaster

George Braithwaite
1746–1812 of Kendal

Joseph 1761–1835
of Bromley Hall
m. Sarah Lloyd
1764–1847

Robert 1754–1827
of Hebblethwaite
Hall

Isaac Braithwaite
1781–1861 of Kendal
m. Anna Lloyd 1788–1859

Anne 1795–1881
m. Richard Janson
1799–1830

Rachel
1788–1862

m. James Foster
1787–1861

Isaac
Braithwaite
1810–1890

Others
(see Table III)

'Foster & Janson'
1825–1833

'Foster & Braithwaite'
1833–

TABLE II—LLOYD

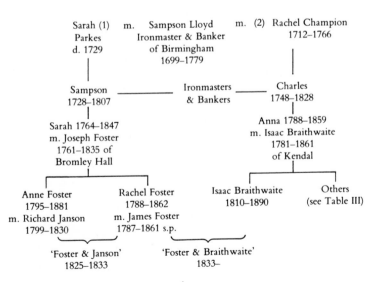

Sarah (1)
Parkes
d. 1729

m. Sampson Lloyd
Ironmaster & Banker
of Birmingham
1699–1779

m. (2) Rachel Champion
1712–1766

Sampson
1728–1807

Ironmasters
& Bankers

Charles
1748–1828

Sarah 1764–1847
m. Joseph Foster
1761–1835 of
Bromley Hall

Anna 1788–1859
m. Isaac Braithwaite
1781–1861
of Kendal

Anne Foster
1795–1881
m. Richard Janson
1799–1830

Rachel Foster
1788–1862
m. James Foster
1787–1861 s.p.

Isaac Braithwaite
1810–1890

Others
(see Table III)

'Foster & Janson'
1825–1833

'Foster & Braithwaite'
1833–

ix

TABLE III—FAMILY PARTNERSHIP

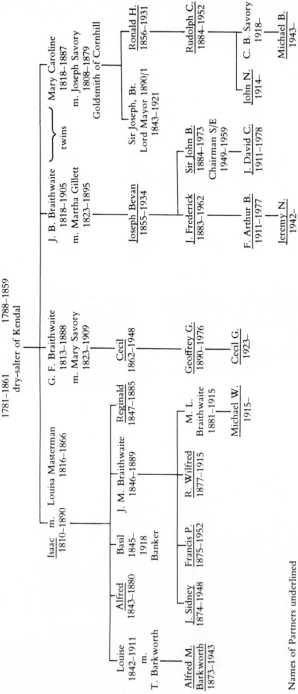

Isaac Braithwaite m. Anna Lloyd
1781–1861   1788–1859
dry-salter of Kendal

Isaac m. Louisa Masterman
1810–1890   1816–1866

G. F. Braithwaite
1813–1888
m. Mary Savory
1823–1909

J. B. Braithwaite
1818–1905
m. Martha Gillett
1823–1895

Mary Caroline
1818–1887
m. Joseph Savory
1808–1879
Goldsmith of Cornhill

} twins

Louise
1842–1911
m.
T. Barkworth

Alfred
1843–1880

Basil
1845–
1918
Banker

J. M. Braithwaite
1846–1889

Reginald
1847–1885

Cecil
1862–1948

Joseph Bevan
1855–1934

Sir Joseph, Bt.
Lord Mayor 1890/1
1843–1921

Ronald H.
1856–1931

Alfred M.
Barkworth
1873–1943

J. Sidney
1874–1948

Francis P.
1875–1952

R. Wilfred
1877–1915

M. L.
Braithwaite
1881–1915

Geoffrey G.
1890–1976

J. Frederick
1883–1962

Sir John B.
1884–1973
Chairman S/E
1949–1959

Rudolph C.
1884–1952

Michael W.
1915–

Cecil G.
1923–

F. Arthur B.
1911–1977

J. David C.
1911–1978

John N.
1914–

C. B. Savory
1918–

Jeremy N.
1942–

Michael B.
1943–

Names of Partners underlined

Chapter I
The Prime Mover

Charles Duguid (1864–1922), a financial journalist of some eminence, wrote of the Stock Exchange in 1900 that it had been 'conceived in a coffee shop and born with the 19th century.'[1] His tone, though genial, is far from respectful. T. H. S. Escott (d. 1924), successor to John Morley as editor of the *Fortnightly Review* and an author widely read in his day, had this to say, in 1879, of the stockbroker, contrasted (much to his disadvantage) with the merchant:

The merchant drives to his place of business in a family brougham or barouche; the stock-broker drives to the station, where he takes the morning express to the City, in a smart dog-cart, with a high-stepping horse between the shafts, and a very knowing-looking groom at his side.... The life of the ideal stockbroker is one of display; that of the ideal merchant, one of dignified grandeur or opulent comfort. Possessed of a certain amount of education, often acquired at a public school, sometimes both at Eton and Oxford, the stock-broker ... has decided social aspirations. He makes his money easily, and he spends it lightly in procuring all the luxuries of existence. He marries a handsome wife, sets up a showy establishment, lays in a stock of choice wines, hires a French cook; he has carriages and horses, a box at the opera, stalls at theatres and concerts innumerable. He belongs to one or two good though not always first-rate clubs. He has acquaintances in the highest circles, and congratulates himself on being in society.[2]

1

Escott, evidently enjoying himself, goes on to refer to the stockbroker's excellent dinner parties, attended by 'young guardsmen and other patrician guests' and to draw a picture of the stockbroker's pretty wife, in consequence, receiving 'a copious stream of male visitors at the residence of the fortunate speculator in scrip and shares, while the lord and master of the household is occupied in the City'. Perhaps, he concludes severely, 'an uncharitable world begins to talk; at any rate, the glitter and show of the *ménage* acquire a certain flavour of Bohemianism, between which and the animating spirit of English society the only sympathy that exists is of a purely superficial kind'.

For Escott, evidently, stockbrokers are suffused with a sinful glamour—the glamour of living dangerously, sexually as well as financially, which he delights in deploring from the safe heights of conventional morality. The root of the matter lies in his description of the stockbroker as a 'fortunate *speculator* in scrip and shares'. Speculation implies gambling: it is this element of gambling, inter-mingled with the solid respectability of providing a market for trading in securities, that has given the Stock Exchange, since its earliest days, a reputation at once dashing and reprehensible which both attracts and repels the mind of the public at large. Perhaps also the minds of members. People are inclined to think of a stockbroker as a bit of a card, and perhaps the stockbroker rather likes it.

Escott, and Duguid after him, were writing at a time when the Stock Exchange, recent though its origins might be, was securely established, expanding rapidly, an accepted feature of the financial landscape, not merely of the City of London but of the world. In its earlier, seedier days its glamour had been less apparent: its sinfulness much more so.

Organised trading in marketable securities in London had its origins in the late 17th century, partly with the rise of joint-stock companies but much more importantly with the methods of war finance which brought a permanent

National Debt into existence. The financial crisis of 1720–1721 which goes by the name of the South Sea Bubble cast the joint-stock principle into deep discredit, and until well into the first quarter of the 19th century 'stock-jobbing'—a phrase full of unsavoury implications—was chiefly a matter of dealings in 'the Funds': that is, British Government securities.[3] For 44 of the 75 years between 1740 and 1815 Great Britain was officially at war: unofficially for several more, so that the National Debt was constantly increasing. The opportunities which it provided both for gambling and for investment gave the Stock Exchange its peculiar reputation.

Gambling arose from the constantly varying price of stock in the market, especially in war time. The Funds, as a writer in the first quarter of the 19th century put it, 'are always much higher in time of peace than in time of war, and are affected by every event, even by every report, in time of war, favourable or unfavourable; and reports are frequently raised by designing people for that very purpose.'[4] Here was a tempting field for the gambler and gamblers have never been scarce in English society. At least as early as the 1690s monied men—and others—had seen the possibilities inherent in backing stocks for rise or fall, and purely speculative activities were going on alongside genuine investment.[5]

Speculative dealings, thus early, began to take two forms which became permanent, prominent and much criticised features of Stock Exchange business, and which we shall come across repeatedly in later chapters of this book. Each represented a bet on the future course of prices. So, in a sense, do dealings for permanent investment, but speculation parts company from investment when the bet becomes the main object of a bargain, as it does when the parties are interested not in the stock which is the nominal object of the transaction but solely in the rise or fall of its price on the market.

One method of betting is to buy an option to take or

deliver stock on some future day at a price fixed when the option is taken, in the hope that before it has to be exercised the price will have risen if stock is to be taken or fallen if it is to be delivered. If the option is not exercised, the money paid for it is lost. An option to deliver stock is called a 'put': to take it, a 'call', and an option to do either is a 'put and call'.

Another practice as old as the Stock Exchange is the gamble of contracting to buy stock one has no intention of holding (and may not have enough money to pay for) or to sell stock one does not possess, in the hope that between the date of striking the bargain and the date it falls due for settlement the price will have moved up if one is a buyer or down if one has agreed to sell. The speculator for the rise (a 'bull') can then meet his obligations by the proceeds of an immediate sale and take a profit, and the speculator for the fall (a 'bear') can buy in enough stock to meet his bargain, sell as agreed, and profit by the difference. As long as the Stock Exchange has been in existence, except during the two great wars of the 20th century and during the economic crisis of 1931, elaborate arrangements have been made to accommodate speculators, and particularly to make it possible for them, at a price, to carry time bargains forward from account to account without, as the case may be, delivering stock which they have contracted to sell or taking possession of stock which they have contracted to buy. The system depends on having a wide and active market, so that the speculator can rely on finding someone who, for a consideration, is willing to take over obligations which he wishes to postpone. It was explained by J. H. Daniell, Government broker, to the Royal Commission of 1877.[6] A seller who did not wish to deliver stock, he said, could borrow it—'the lender of the stock allows the person with whom he is bargaining to have his stock transferred to the original buyer'. A buyer, on the other hand, who did not want to take delivery, would find a dealer willing to do so, charging interest on the money needed for the purchase. 'That is called "contangoing", is it not?' asked a member of the Royal Commission. 'Yes, or "continuation",' Daniell replied. There is lucrative business to be had in lending the money or stock needed for continuations, and a reasonably skillful or lucky speculator can operate with very little capital, since bargains match each other and settlements can be arrived at by the payment of differences.

The transactions in contango operations are in essence bogus, since a bull agrees to buy stock which he does not want and a bear agrees to sell stock which he does not own. For that reason, in the early 18th century, an attempt was made to legislate this kind of speculation out of existence. In 1734, under a statute which came to be known as Sir John Barnard's Act, time bargains which were purely speculative, as distinct from genuine investors' bargains, were made illegal.

Sir John Barnard (1685–1764), a wine merchant, was Lord Mayor of London in 1737 and MP for the City nearly forty years (1722–1761). He was formidable enough in Parliament to worry Sir Robert Walpole and he was a leading authority on public finance. He married his daughter into the aristocracy, albeit Irish, and thus became great-grandfather to one of Queen Victoria's most famous, though least favoured, Prime Ministers: the third Viscount Palmerston (1784–1865). When it is added that he started life as a Quaker but switched at eighteen into the Church of England, it will be seen that he is a very worthy example of that perennial figure on the English social scene: the business man rising commercially, politically and socially. 'Sir John Barnard', as his 19th-century biographer put it, 'was the type of an honourable British merchant in his day,'[7] and it was the type which, over 100 years after Sir John's death, Escott still esteemed far more highly than the typical stockbroker. It may be imagined how greatly Barnard may have disapproved of the stockbrokers of his own day: that homeless band, of very mixed social, commercial and ethnic origins, who did their business not in the ordered decency of a counting-house like his own, but in the coffee–houses and even the alleyways of the City.

Barnard's opinion, and no doubt orthodox City opinion of his day, is made pretty plain in the title of the Act associated with his name: 'An Act to prevent the infamous Practice of Stock-jobbing.' It was not aimed at time-bargains as such, which were part of the normal machinery of investment, but at bargains not based on any genuine intention to hold stock when it was bought or to dispose of stock already held. It referred to 'wagers and contracts in the nature of wagers' and to 'contracts relating to the ... present or future price or value of ... stock or securities', and it declared them 'null and void'. It provided a penalty of £500 for entering into bargains of this sort, and it forbade the payment of premiums for taking up options. It forbade also, again under heavy penalties, the 'frequent and mischievous practice for persons to sell and dispose of stocks or securities of which they are not possessed', and it required all bargains to be settled by the actual delivery of stock and the actual payment of cash. Settlement by paying or receiving differences was specifically forbidden.[8]

The Act was intended to destroy the entire system of speculative time bargains which seems to have been so offensive to the 18th-century conscience. It quite failed to do so, and instead of straightening out the morality of Stock Exchange dealings the Act made it more tortuous than ever.

This was because it is one thing to pass an Act and quite another to enforce it against the people it chiefly affects if they are not minded to obey, especially if they are banded together in a way that makes disobedience effective. 18th-century speculators were not at all minded to give up time-bargains just because Parliament had seen fit to legislate against them, nor were brokers inclined to give up the business which speculation provided. Everyone concerned in the illegal transactions had a common interest in seeing that they did not come to light and no doubt they had means of discouraging informers on whom Barnard's Act, like many other 18th-century Acts, largely relied for enforcement.

Barnard's Act did not stop speculative bargains, but it did prevent aggrieved parties from going to law to enforce them, since obviously the courts would not recognise a bargain which was itself illegal. If a speculating client refused to pay his debts, his broker had no redress in law, nor could brokers proceed against each other. The Act, indeed, placed speculative debts in the same position as other gambling debts: they were secured only on the good faith of those incurring them and had no legal force behind them.

They were backed instead by the common interest of all who dealt in the stock market, especially the brokers. Whatever conduct might be tolerated, even expected, in other matters, it was essential that in the keeping of stock market bargains those who made them should be utterly trustworthy, and the penalty for breach of trust was exclusion from the market, which for a speculator would mean no more speculation and for a broker the loss of his business.*

Members of the Stock Exchange have long taken pride in this code of conduct, unsupported by any force of law and largely independent of written undertakings, which distinguishes their calling. It is ironical that so strict a rule of honourable behaviour should have had some part, at least, of its origins in the inconvenient consequences of setting the law at defiance. Barnard's Act was progressively whittled down, by judgments in the courts, until at length

---

*This, in the 18th century, might not have been so serious as it would have been later, since until the early part of the 19th century stockbrokers might carry on other businesses as well, though after February 1812 no new members were admitted to the Stock Exchange who did so.[9]

it came to be regarded as governing only transactions in British Government securities. Nevertheless it was not repealed until 1867. For over 130 years, therefore, while the Stock Exchange was arising from its rather squalid 18th-century obscurity to its mid-19th-century eminence, some of its most characteristic activities were technically illegal and many, if not all, of its most respected members must have been habitual breakers of the law. They broke the law with the most scrupulous regard for their illegal obligations, and the paradox goes a long way to account for the Stock Exchange's equivocal reputation.

The 18th-century background to the practice and reputation of the Stock Exchange has been discussed at some length because it set the tone for the 19th century and later, which is the period we are chiefly interested in. Let us not pretend that we are concerned with an institution preoccupied mainly with sober investment and only incidentally with speculation. We are not. We are concerned with an institution far less grave and reverend. A large part of stock market business has always been speculative and that has been recognised, as we have seen, as long as there have been any organised dealings in publicly quoted securities. Whether speculation is deplored as sinful gambling or admired as spirited risk-taking, it is a prime mover in the stock market.

REFERENCES

1 Charles Duguid, 'The History of the Stock Exchange', p. 1, W. Eden Hooper (ed.), *The Stock Exchange in the Year 1900*, Spottiswoode & Co., n.d.
2 T. H. S. Escott, *England, its People, Polity and Pursuits*, 2 vols, Cassell, Petter, Galpin & Co., n.d. (1879?), II, pp. 40–42.
3 E. Victor Morgan and W. A. Thomas, *The Stock Exchange, its History and Functions*, Elek Books, 1962, Chapters 1 and 2.
4 Anon., *A New Guide to the Public Funds and Every Man his Own Stockbroker*, D. B. Woodward, n.d. (1825?).

5 As (3), pp. 20–21.
6 QQ 630–641 in Minutes of Evidence of the London Stock Exchange Commission, C2157/1878, HC Papers XIX 1878.
7 W. P. Courtenay (1845–1913) in DNB.
8 As (1), p. 36; as (3), pp. 62–63.
9 As (3), pp. 75–77.

Chapter II
The Stock Exchange and the Economy about 1825

The Stock Exchange of the early 19th century, with its questionable moral climate, might not seem to be the most obvious place of business for members of the Society of Friends, and there is no evidence that they were very numerous in 'the House'. Nevertheless in 1825 two Quaker brothers-in-law, James Foster and Richard Janson, went into partnership to found a firm which, as Foster & Braithwaite, has survived into the 1970s with a collection of records, including an unbroken run of books of account, which make it possible to approach Stock Exchange history from the standpoint of one of the member firms. This chapter will survey the general background to the firm's foundation, in the Stock Exchange and further afield. In Chapter III we shall return in greater detail to Foster & Braithwaite's origins.

In 1825 the Stock Exchange had been in its own building, put up at the expense of the 550 original members, since 1802. It was a private institution in the old English fashion, like Lloyd's and the Inns of Court—that is to say, a private institution with considerable public responsibilities—and it ran its own affairs with very little in the way of control from outside. To the great annoyance of members, the Corporation of the City of London had an ancient right to insist on brokers swearing an oath, paying fees, and finding guarantors for good behaviour before they could legally ply their trade, but by the 19th century any control the City might have exercised had lapsed. Moreover there were always brokers who evaded their obligations to swear and pay, and jobbers were never under any: a reason, it has been suggested, why the differentiation of functions developed.[1] For practical purposes, including the observance of the law of the land as expressed in Barnard's Act, the members of the Stock Exchange governed themselves through their elected Committee for General Purposes; through the rule book, issued for the first time in 1812; and through their own sense of proper behaviour.

The regular members of the Stock Exchange, with their 'House', their settled constitution and their rules, written and unwritten, were in a strong position, but they had no monopoly. Outside brokers, numerous when the first Stock Exchange was built, were active throughout the 19th century, though the supporters of the Stock Exchange, for obvious reasons, continually cast doubt on their respectability. 'I ... found myself in a spacious apartment', wrote a non-member in 1828, '... nearly filled with persons more respectable in appearance'—he means the members—'than the crew I had left at the door.'[2] The comparison favours the members, but only just.

Jobbers, or dealers, buy and sell on their own account, making their profit from 'the dealer's turn'—the difference between buying and selling prices—which they earn by supplying stock to meet the demands of the market. Brokers deal with jobbers on behalf of their clients, charging commission for their services. The two functions had long been recognised when the Stock Exchange moved into its own building in 1802, but it is doubtful whether members were compelled, as they later were, to do the one thing or the other, but not both.

These early 19th-century jobbers and brokers carried on their business in a country well on the way to becoming what Professor Mathias has called 'the first industrial nation',[3] but in 1825 the process was still far from complete. The United Kingdom's population of about 21 million, of whom nearly 7 million were in Ireland, was growing very fast: indeed a 'population explosion' was going on which would carry the figure for the United Kingdom from less than 16 million at the time of the first Census—1801—to just over 27 million in 1851 and 41.5 million by the end of the century.[4] Many economists in the first quarter of the nineteenth century, led by Professor T. R. Malthus (1766–1834) of Haileybury College, had grave doubts whether population growing so fast could ever be adequately fed.

British society in 1825, for all the profound changes which were occurring, was still a society in which land was the major source of wealth, the most secure investment for capital, much the most important base for social standing and political power, and the largest single source of livelihood, for agriculture employed more people than any other activity and until about 1850 most people lived in villages and the countryside, not in large towns. For centuries it had been possible to make a fortune in trade, and it was becoming possible to make one in manufacturing industry, but the instinct—a very sound one—of the successful business man was to put his money, once made, into land, both for the social consequences and very agreeable way of life which a landed estate carried with it and from motives of prudence—land was a much, much safer investment than any kind of commercial or industrial activity. The great landowners at the top of society were very rich indeed: far richer, almost certainly, than even the most successful business men. By 1790, Professor F. M. L. Thompson tells us, such grandees as the Dukes of Bedford, Bridgewater, Devonshire or Northumberland 'could comfortably dispose of over £50,000 a year',[5] and as the economic life of the country quickened those who had property in London or in other growing towns, or in mining districts, grew even richer.

The owner of a landed estate did not look upon it pri-

12

marily as a commercial undertaking, but as the necessary base for what a 17th-century epitaph calls 'the port of his Quality'.[6] Nevertheless if he were business-like he would seek to improve it by enclosure, by shrewd management, by equally shrewd marriage, and perhaps by such ventures as the Bridgewater Canal (built by the Duke of Bridge-water in 1759–1761) or the Lilleshall Company, founded in the 18th century by the Leveson-Gower family, later Earls of Granville, to exploit the ironstone on their land in Shropshire. None of these activities, even when they were directly commercial or industrial in character, rather than agricultural, brought business directly to the Stock Exchange, although they certainly did a great deal for the economic development of the country.

Apart from land or houses built on it (the phrase 'safe as houses' presumably has financial origins), the safest home for an investor's money was in 'the Funds': that is to say, the various stocks which represented Government borrowing, overwhelmingly for warlike purposes, since the late 17th century. The investor had a variety of Government stocks to choose from, and alongside them there were East India stocks. The British Government's issues had been consolidated in 1817 into four main classes with coupons between 3 per cent and 5 per cent.[7] The stock most widely held was 'Three per cent. Consolidated Annuities': the majestic 'Consols' of Victorian England. In all the years between 1825 and 1914 the yield on consols only rose as high as 4 per cent in two years—1825 itself and 1826—and normally it was a shade over 3 per cent except during the '90s and a few years early in the 20th century when it dropped a little under: several times as low as 2.4 per cent:[8] The security of the Funds for the long-term investor, as distinct from the speculator, could hardly have been more solid.

The kind of people who sought this solid security were those whose livelihood depended, in whole or in part, on private means which they had neither the inclination nor the competence to employ in business, which would be more profitable but also far more risky. Widows come to mind, and retired officers (who had no pensions until after 1870), and country parsons, and unmarried ladies of advancing years: all the supporting cast in the great Victorian drama, Family Life. Some would hold investments in their own right: others would be beneficiaries of family trusts and marriage settlements.

The Census of 1841, which was the first to attempt a detailed investigation of occupations, recorded 511,440 'independent persons so returned', or about 2.7 per cent of the population of Great Britain. The Census of 1851, going further, recorded 23,032 men and 121,222 women as 'annuitants': probably a fairly close approximation to the number of people wholly or mainly dependent on 'the Funds', as distinct from those who had a holding along with other, possibly larger, sources of income.[9] All these stockholders would have come from time to time to the Stock Exchange, acting either independently or through trustees, attorneys ('men of business'), or bankers, and their activities show up, in the books of Foster & Braithwaite. 'The regular payment of interest on the Government Funds,' says a writer of about 1825, 'and the number of persons who prefer the interest they yield to the hazardous profits obtained from trade, occasion the continual purchases of the various shares that are exposed to sale on the market.'[10]

The Census Commissioners of 1841 were at pains to point out that those returned as independent persons 'are not merely the wealthy, or even those in easy circumstances', and went on to say that the return included 'in the more rural districts many poor widows or aged men living upon their savings'. This is what one would expect on general grounds, and it is borne out by an analysis of the dividends payable on 3 per cent Consols on 5th January 1852. As the table opposite shows, 81 per cent of the dividend payments were for sums up to £50, and nearly 50 per cent were for sums up to £10. This is not conclusive evidence, of course, that all those who received these dividends were small investors. Many may have had income from property or other classes of Government stock. Nevertheless it strongly reinforces the supposition that Consols, along with other Government stocks, were widely held by people of slender means who had to be careful where they put their money.

Dividends payable on 3 per cent Consols on 5th January 1852

Number of dividends		per cent
39,934 not above £5		33.5
17,685	£10	14.8
39,377	£50	33.0
10,986	£100	9.2
6,905	£200	5.8
1,998	£300	1.7
1,409	£500	1.2
613	£1,000	
175	£2,000	0.8
78 over	£2,000	
119,160		100.0

Adapted from 'Classified Table of Stock Proprietors' on p. 35 of Francis Playford, *Practical Hints for investing Money*, London, 6th Edn., 1869.

The other classes of stock listed by Playford, with the number of dividends payable, are:

Dividends payable 10 October 1851:

3 per cent Reduced Annuities	37,016
3¼ per cent Reduced Annuities	95,786
Long Annuities	10,774
Annuities for Terms of Years	2,367

Dividends payable 5 January 1852:

3 per cent Annuities of 1726	351
New 5 per cent Annuities	255
Annuities for Terms of Years	2,482

Although Consols were so important to so many individuals, the largest holders were not private investors but banks (including the Bank of England), insurance companies and Government departments, and their importance was all the greater in the early part of the 19th century when the range of tolerably sound securities was much narrower than it became later on. So steady was the value of Consols, except at the worst moments of financial panic, and so easily and rapidly could they be converted into cash, that for most purposes they could be looked upon as money: that was why they were so attractive to the banks, who could treat holdings of Consols as liquid reserves.[11]

Bank of England stock and East India Company stock might perhaps be regarded, along with 'the Funds', as reasonably safe investments. Outside this class, until the stocks and shares of the larger home railways began to settle down in the late '40s, investment in most Stock Exchange securities was very hazardous indeed, being far more a matter for the professional speculator, not overburdened with scruples, than for the man of moderate means seeking safety rather than excitement. Foreign loans and foreign mining, in the 1820s and 1830s—and later—were notorious, and company promotion, such as it was at this time, fully justified the dark suspicion in which corporate enterprise was widely held. Finance for commerce and industry at home, generally speaking, did not come near the Stock Exchange. Why this should have been, in the expanding economy of the leading commercial and industrial country of the world, and technically the most advanced, requires examination.

In the first place the law, backed widely by public opinion, heavily discouraged incorporation for business purposes and especially incorporation with limited liability. In 1720, during the speculative ferment leading up to the 'South Sea Bubble', an Act had been passed which, like some other Acts, had a limited purpose—the promotion of the interests of two insurance companies—immediately in view, but very wide and long-lasting effects.[12] The Bubble Act, as it became known, contained clauses which meant that companies could only be incorporated, and shares in them could only be legally transferable, after processes leading up to the grant of letters patent or of a Royal Charter, or to a private Act. These processes were costly, lengthy, and open to opposition every step of the way. Incorporation was impossible for small or middling-sized businesses, and in practice it was reserved for undertakings which needed large capital raised in advance. In the 18th and early 19th century companies were incorporated for insurance and for a range of public utilities—canals, docks, waterworks and gasworks, roads and bridges—but not for manufacturing or commerce, although in commerce two venerable oddities, the East India Company and the Hudson's Bay Company, survived from a much earlier age. Until the railways came, the market for shares in private enterprise was narrow and unimportant by comparison with the market for Government stock.

It is hardly likely that this situation was entirely the result of the Bubble Act. There were ways round it, but they were not very much used, and there was no very insistent call for its repeal. Nevertheless, as the 19th century advanced, the demand for incorporation by Act of Parliament grew, and in 1825, largely to relieve pressure on parliamentary time, the Bubble Act was repealed, making the road to incorporation and limited liability slightly easier. Even so, there was no great rush along it, except briefly in 1825 itself. Respectable business men, then and for many years afterwards were inclined, with some reason, to regard company promotion as the work, if not of the Devil, then of financiers and stockbrokers quite closely related to him, and limited liability as a method of cheating one's creditors.

The traditional method of organising a business of any

kind, whether it was to run a cotton mill, a bank, a sur-
geon's practice, a stockbroker's office, or any other kind
of undertaking, was on the basis of absolute ownership and
unlimited liability, borne either by one man or a group
of partners who alone or collectively supplied the capital.
Businesses of this kind, as we shall see in the case of Foster
& Braithwaite, were kept very carefully within a circle of
relations by blood or marriage, and only in very unusual
circumstances would an outsider be admitted. Nepotism,
intelligently administered, was looked upon as the right
and natural way of choosing owners and managers for the
family firm, and throughout the 19th century—and
beyond—the family firm remained by far the commonest
unit of business organisation: certainly it was so in 1825.[13]

Family firms had no use for the Stock Exchange. They
raised fixed capital, just as they found partners and successors, among friends and relations. For working capital
they depended on the banks (sometimes also for longer-
term investment) and on the mechanism of credit, already
highly developed, which was founded on discounting bills
of exchange. Nearly everything depended on personal
knowledge and trust: the idea of 'going public' would
have seemed strange, distasteful, a betrayal not only of
business principles but of family loyalties.

In the 1820s, in any case, the demand for capital for long-
term investment on a large scale was comparatively small,
except in the public utilities which we have already
glanced at. The merchant had scarcely yet been displaced
by the factory owner from his immemorial position of
dominance in the business world, and unless he was a great
ship-owner his main need was for working capital, not
fixed investment. On the industrial side cotton mills
employing several hundred 'hands' were already fairly
common, and in some other industries—iron-working,
brewing, ship-building are examples—there were a few
undertakings on the same scale as the larger ones in cotton.
In general, however, the British economy was not yet

based on large factories or mechanised production: rather on small masters, outwork, hand craftsmanship; and the outlines of the later industrial society were only barely beginning to form. In particular, the great streams of factory-made consumer goods and of imported foodstuffs which were to make life so much easier for the mass of the population two or three generations later, and equally to call for massive capital investment at home and abroad, were scarcely even thought of.

This is the Homeric age of emerging industrial capitalism: rough, hard, pitiless, full of heroic figures and memorable strife: a prolific begetter of myth and legend still potent a century and a half later. For the business man, particularly the small man struggling to hoist himself and his family into security and affluence, it was a world full of risk and recurrent disaster. If masters combined to keep their men in poverty or near it, it was often because they were not far away from it themselves, and a year or two of bad trade or a commercial crisis could tip them over into it.

Commercial crises struck the business world with dismal rhythmic periodicity: 1797, 1816, 1825–1826, 1836–1837, 1847–1848, 1857–1858, 1866 are some of the more notorious years. Each produced its tale of crashing banks, insolvent merchants, manufacturers forced to close, and a general slowing down of activity with its repercussions down and down the scale to the 'labouring poor' at the bottom. It is noteworthy that these lamentable occurrences were seen by contemporaries as *commercial*—not *industrial*—crises. The merchant was still king, or considered to be so, and the manufacturer was a secondary figure.

For the business man with unlimited liability but whose access to capital and credit, even at the top of the tree, had very tight limits indeed, disaster was never entirely out of sight or out of mind, no matter how eminent his position and the position of his firm. D. Morier Evans (1819–1874), the contemporary historian of the crisis of 1847–1848, observed 'as a curious fact' that since 1830 'no less than six' prominent City men, each of whom had served as Deputy Governor of the Bank of England, had failed, and among those who failed in that particular crisis was Sir John Rae Reid, Governor of the Bank of England in 1839 and a senior Director when his firm, Reid Irving & Co., stopped payment.[14] Bankruptcy, indeed, might merely be an incident—painful, no doubt, but passing—in an otherwise successful career, and by taking on a new, solvent, partner it was fairly easy to put a firm which had suspended payment back into business again. 'It is singular', remarks Morier Evans, 'with what facility new firms are organized after old ones have broken down, and paid, probably, a few shillings in the pound.'[15] No doubt, but it would have needed a thickish skin and steady nerves, both very necessary items of equipment in early—and not so early—19th-century business life.

The Stock Exchange had grown up with one of the most important financial devices of the 18th century: the National Debt, which in the first quarter of the 19th century still provided most of its business. In the emerging industrial economy there seemed to be no very central part for it to play, either in raising capital or in providing a market for securities. With the building of the railways, requiring far more capital than a private partnership could conceivably supply, and with the immense broadening, as time went on, of the field of overseas investment, the scene would alter dramatically and profoundly, but in 1825 those developments were yet to come. When Foster & Janson first went into business as brokers, the first industrial nation, though struggling to be born, had scarcely as yet come to birth.

REFERENCES

1 Morgan & Thomas, p. 66.
2 John Francis, *Chronicles and Characters of the Stock Exchange*, Longmans, 1855, p. 330.

3 Peter Mathias, *The First Industrial Nation*, Methuen, 1969.
4 As (3), p. 449; see also B. R. Mitchell and Phyllis Deane, *Abstract of British Historical Statistics*, CUP, 1962, pp. 6–7.
5 F. M. L. Thompson, *English Landed Society in the Nineteenth Century*, Routledge & Kegan Paul, 1963, p. 25.
6 Epitaph to John, 3rd Earl of Bristol, in Sherborne Abbey.
7 Morgan & Thomas, p. 113.
8 Morgan & Thomas, pp. 278–279.
9 *The Companion to the Almanac . . . for 1845*, Charles Knight, n.d. (1846?), pp. 42, 93; Report of the Census of 1851.
10 *A new Guide to the Public Funds*, p. 4.
11 Morgan & Thomas, pp. 118–123.
12 Barry Supple, *The Royal Exchange Assurance*, CUP, 1970, pp. 32–33; Morgan & Thomas, pp. 37–8; Mathias, p. 162.
13 Mathias, p. 162.
14 D. Morier Evans, *The Commercial Crisis 1847–1848*, 2nd Edn, 1849, David & Charles Reprints, 1969, pp. 47–48, 68, 72.
15 D. Morier Evans, *The History of the Commercial Crisis 1857–1858*, London, 1859, David & Charles Reprints 1969, pp. 57–58, 28n; see also p. 52.

Chapter III
Quakers in Partnership:
the Foundation of Foster &
Braithwaite

Of James Foster (1787–1861) and Richard Janson (d. 1830) we do not know a great deal, but two of the things we do know are important. First, at the time when they went into partnership they were both members of the Society of Friends. Secondly, they had married sisters whose mother was a daughter of Sampson Lloyd (1728–1807), one of the four original partners in Taylors & Lloyds, the first banking firm set up in Birmingham (1765) and the ancestor of Lloyds Bank.[1]

As Quakers, Foster and Janson belonged to what was possibly the most influential, wealthiest and closest-knit group in the business life of the day. As husbands, they were connected with one of the greatest Quaker families: the Lloyds. The life of the Quakers, rather like the life of the Jews, revolved in complicated, inter-connected patterns of activity about three central considerations: religion, family, business. The formation of the new partnership was part of that pattern. Let us stand back for a moment and look at it.

Religious persecution of the more savage kind ceased to seem desirable to most Englishmen, except in isolated moments of frenzy, towards the end of the 17th century. Nevertheless until well on in the 19th century it remained necessary to be a communicant member of the Church of England to qualify for the full rights of citizenship, and no one could be in the mainstream of politics, university

life, or the service of the Crown who would not outwardly
conform to Church observances. Many worthy people did
not find the strain on their consciences intolerable, but de-
vout Quakers, among others, did. As a consequence they
remained, along with Roman Catholics, Jews, Unitarians
and the older sects of Dissent, always set apart: tolerated
but unwelcome, and liable from time to time, as minorities
always are, to feel the weight of the majority's dislike.

The Quakers' equivocal standing in the eye of the law
and in public opinion did not stop them from prospering
in business, any more than it stopped other Dissenters and
Unitarians. Perhaps it positively helped. It shut off some
routes to worldly well-being—particularly, in the 18th
century, Church preferment, Crown employment and the
lucrative ramifications of the law—but it enforced single-
minded concentration on what was left, which in an
expanding economy was by no means a narrow or an un-
rewarding field.

Quaker principles presented no obstacle to getting rich:
indeed, far from it. They emphasised precisely those
virtues of hard work and plain living which might be
expected to contribute to business success. Moreover they
insisted on honest dealing which produced trading
partners whom suppliers, customers and creditors, not
themselves Quakers, could readily trust.

Going further, there was evidently no matter of
conscience standing between a Quaker and speculation.
Professor Mathias, in his study of the history of English
brewing, came across Peter Briggins, a Quaker of the early
18th century, who dealt in hops, honey, wax and tobacco
'in addition to his main dealings on the Exchange in the
Funds'. Briggins, 'the true speculator buying only for a
rise and resale to the same groups from whom he purchased', recorded his transactions alongside notes of 'the
philanthropic strivings of his fellow-Quakers to redeem
their time on earth, and ... between the out-pourings
of his self-communicated homilies.'[2] From this kind of

business, conducted chiefly in pubs and coffee-houses, it would be no distance at all to the business of a stockbroker, and if the one activity could be reconciled with conscience, why not the other? We shall not find the partners in Foster & Braithwaite in the least averse to speculative dealings.

There were not, in fact, many branches of trade or industry which the Society of Friends collectively disapproved of. Their pacifist principles barred them from the making of weapons, though not from producing iron from which cannon could be cast, nor is there much evidence of refusal to profit indirectly from wartime demand, which would have made life very difficult in the 18th century. On the contrary there is some evidence of positively welcoming wartime opportunities as, for instance, demand for non-ferrous metals during the Seven Years' War.[3] The distilling of spirits was not a trade for a respectable 18th century Quaker, but brewing was. Beer was a necessary article of diet, not an encouragement to vice.[4] That view of it came later, but by then beer drinkers had rather more money to spend and the water supplies had improved.

The limitations, such as they were, on Quakers' business activities were not very crippling, and they applied themselves to a wide variety of occupations. During the 18th century they were strong in corn, in iron and in brewing, and during the early part of the 19th century they advanced into two of the newer food trades: factory-made biscuits and chocolate. In the conditions of the 18th century, any firm with a good name and in a fair way of business could very easily take on some of the functions of a bank, particularly in accepting money on deposit and in negotiating bills of exchange. Quaker firms, perhaps because their credit was exceptionally sound, seem to have been especially well placed to move into banking, and in the later part of the 18th century when banks, properly so-called, were being set up throughout the country,

Quakers became very prominent indeed in the partnerships that ran them.[5]

The high standing of Quakers in the business community was backed by a discipline which spread outwards from matters of faith to every aspect of life, including the conduct of business. A Friend who had the misfortune to go bankrupt might expect to have his affairs narrowly scrutinised and no lenient view taken. When Charles Lloyd of Dolobran, an ironmaster and a member of a highly respected Quaker family, came to grief through over-trading in 1730 he was formally disowned by the Yearly Meeting for Wales and admonished 'to make such restitution to the many sufferers that he has injured as may convince the world of his being in some degree on that foundation which alone can reconcile him to God and with his people'.[6]

The importance of bankers in a growing economy needs no emphasis, and the influence of the Quakers in the business life of the country, in this and in other occupations, was out of all proportion to their numbers. Exact figures are impossible to come by, but at the beginning of the 18th century, when the population of Great Britain was perhaps about 7 million, there may have been some 60,000 Quakers. By the time the first Census was taken, in 1801, the population of Great Britain was about 10.5 million, but the number of Quakers had been cut, largely by expulsion for marriage outside the Society and by a general tightening of discipline, to about 20,000, or rather less than 0.2 per cent.[7]

These 20,000 were scattered widely about the country. Nevertheless they formed a highly self-conscious group, and a group small enough for many of its members to know each other, the more readily since Quakers travelled indefatigably for purposes of religion and of business. Marriage outside the Society of Friends was severely discouraged, and as a consequence the entire Society, from one end of the country to the other, was criss-crossed by an intricate web of family relationships, assiduously traced out and recorded by generation after generation of genealogists.

Quaker marriages were not as a rule undertaken on any grounds so flimsy as romantic love. They were arranged with an eye to property and to business, and business among the Quakers was even more intensely a family affair than in the generality of the population. Here we return very close to the heart of our subject, for the first three partners in the firm which started as Foster & Janson and quickly became Foster & Braithwaite were related to each other by connections with the great Birmingham family of Lloyd.

Before looking at the marriages, it will be worth while casting a glance at James Foster's parentage, which was unusual for a Quaker since his father Robert Foster (1754–1827) had been briefly a lieutenant in the Navy. As a very young man indeed he had gone to Antigua as a storekeeper for his grandfather Myles Birkett, a West India merchant, and he must have had some sea training, for which the American war broke out in 1776 he joined H.M.S. *Endeavour* to cruise against privateers and very swiftly became a lieutenant. In 1779, after service in several other vessels and command of one, he came home to Lancaster, where he caused a stir in the Quaker meeting house by appearing there in uniform. 'I hope he will earn preferment and be a credit to the place,' commented the Vicar of Lancaster, adding acidly: 'as well as an example to some others of that society to break through the principle established by them to enjoy all the advantages of peace, but to leave it to others to fight the battles.' [8]

Whether Robert Foster in early life was a Quaker seems doubtful. Robert Southey, writing in 1806, remarked that he 'had turned Quaker or semi-Quaker'. At any rate, after shocking the Lancaster Friends he was reconciled to them, married a Quaker girl, Mary Burton, and settled at Hebblethwaite Hall on Cartmel Fell. Presumably his cruising had been profitable or his wife brought him money. He went into business as a woolspinner and cloth manufacturer, moved to Newcastle-upon-Tyne some time before 1821, and died there in 1827. Southey, who met him through an introduction from Wordsworth, was much taken with him. 'He looked a first assassin Macbeth as to his costume—but he was a rare man. He had been a lieutenant in the Navy; was scholar enough to quote Virgil aptly....'[9]

Of Richard Janson's family background we know nothing. It seems reasonable, however, to suppose that he was connected with one of the partners in the London banking house of Brown, Janson. They were bankers to the partners in Foster & Braithwaite in later years and they did much business with the firm.

The girls whom James Foster and Richard Janson married were, respectively, Rachel and Ann, daughters of Joseph and Sarah Foster who, according to the Dictionary of Quaker Biography at Friends' House, 'lived in state at Bromley Hall in Middlesex'. Joseph Foster was a calico printer, and no doubt a prosperous one, but what had probably contributed as much as anything to his stateliness was his marriage to the eldest daughter of Sampson Lloyd of Birmingham. That brought him close to the centre of a network in which business partnerships and marriage partnerships—intricately intermingled, all within the Society of Friends—ramified profitably through coal mining, iron mining, iron and (after Joseph's time) steel production, and banking. His sons-in-law would take their place in that network, too.[10]

The coal and iron interests arose from a Lloyd inheritance of mineral rights and land near Wednesbury. The way in which they were dealt with is a very good example of the way in which marriage and business were interwoven, keeping all within the Religious Society of Friends. Joseph Foster and his brother-in-law, Samuel Lloyd (1768–1849), were executors of the will of Sampson

Lloyd, and in pursuance of its intentions they encouraged the setting up of a firm which became Lloyds Fosters & Company. The original partners included two of Joseph Foster's sons and two of Samuel Lloyd's. For nearly fifty years the firm was prosperous and enterprising, but in 1862 the partners of the day entered into commitments, connected with the building of Blackfriars Bridge in London, which drained away their working capital, and in 1867 the undertaking was sold to the Patent Shaft & Axletree Company of Wednesbury. Even Quaker magic was not entirely sufficient against the precariousness of business life, but it seems to have averted the worst. The senior partner in Lloyds Fosters became Vice-Chairman of Patent Shaft and another partner, his nephew, launched a tube-making business which eventually became Stewarts & Lloyds.[11]

We are more closely concerned with the banking side of the Lloyd family interests. They began in 1765 with the foundation of Taylors & Lloyds, the first bank established in Birmingham. It emerged, as many another bank did, from the banker-like activities previously carried on by businesses run by the families of the founding partners. Of these there were at first four, a father and a son from each side. The Lloyd partners were Sampson Lloyd II (1699–1779) and Sampson Lloyd III, father of Sarah Foster, who was a baby about twelve months old when the bank opened.

Every country bank needed a London agent. In 1770, only five years after they started, Taylors & Lloyds founded their own: a remarkable demonstration of self-confidence. One of the founders of the new London bank was Osgood Hanbury, a wealthy tobacco-broker. In 1757 he had married Sampson Lloyd's younger half-sister Mary (1736–1770), so that once again a marriage alliance and a business partnership were intertwined. In 1790 Sampson Hanbury, a son of the marriage, became a partner in another Quaker enterprise: Trumans' Brewery.[12] Lloyd connections in Quaker banking and Quaker brewing luxuriated. A couple of years after Taylors & Lloyds was founded, Mary Hanbury's sister Rachel (1743–1792) married David Barclay. He was in partnership with his father, an American merchant of such standing that in 1761 he had been visited by George III.[13] He was also a partner in the banking house of Freame & Barclay (his father's second wife was Priscilla Freame), ancestor of Barclays Bank and in 1781 he became one of the proprietors of Barclay Perkins' Brewery. Through the Barclay marriage the Lloyd connections, already wide, widened still further—indeed, bewilderingly so—and among the banking families with whom they became linked were the Gurneys and the Hoares. The financial interplay between Quaker bankers and Quaker brewers, as intricate as the marriage relationships and as profitable, has been traced in detail by Professor Mathias.[14]

These interlocking business and family relationships, as time passed, spread and grew stronger. Private banking was a risky trade, and the successive financial crises of the late 18th and early 19th centuries knocked over many a house of previously unquestioned soundness, but the Lloyds and their allies survived and prospered, requiring as they did so the services of a growing number of members of the owning families. Among the Lloyds there was no lack of potential recruits. Sampson Lloyd II (1699–1779), twice married, left six married children, from whom sprang 44 grandchildren and 120 great-grandchildren.[15]

When Sampson Lloyd II died, in 1779, he left his share in Taylors & Lloyds equally between two sons of his second marriage, Nehemiah (1746–1801) and Charles (1748–1828), thus bringing them into the banking partnership alongside his much older son by his first marriage, Sampson III (1728–1807), who had been a partner from the start. In the next generation, two daughters of Charles and one of Sampson III's sons (he had seventeen children) married two brothers and a sister of the family of Braithwaite at Kendal.[16]

29

George (1777–1853) and Isaac (1781–1861) Braithwaite and their sister Rachel (1768–1854) belonged to a family which had owned a drysaltery* and dyeing business in Kendal since the early 18th century. It required, says a later Braithwaite, 'close attention and considerable knowledge of practical science to realize even moderate profits for the support of two families [ie: the families of George and Isaac]'[16] and it is clear that the Braithwaites, though no doubt comfortable enough, were by no means so wealthy as the Lloyds. They were highly respected, however, in the Society of Friends, and they were cultured, being friendly with Wordsworth, Coleridge and Southey as well as being better acquainted with the sciences than they might have been if they had been brought up in the schools and universities of the Establishment. Isaac Braithwaite himself had gone to the Friends' School in Kendal, being taught there by John Dalton, who became an assistant master in 1781 and was Principal from 1785 to 1793.[17]

Two sons of Sampson Lloyd III—Sampson IV (1765–1800) and Samuel (1768–1849), whom we have already met (p. 27)—were boarders at this school, and perhaps that is how the Lloyds and the Braithwaites came to know each other. In 1796 Samuel married Rachel Braithwaite. The family friendship ripened, and in 1806 and 1808 George and Isaac Braithwaite, partners with their father in the drysaltery, married respectively Mary and Anna, two of the fifteen children of Sampson Lloyd III's much younger half-brother Charles, known as 'Charles Lloyd the Banker' to distinguish him from his son 'Charles Lloyd the Poet'.[18]

We are chiefly concerned with Isaac and his redoubtable wife Anna (1788–1859). 'My heart', she said of herself, 'panted after the Lord. I felt my inward corruption. I saw the hidden things of darkness there.' This was at the age

*'Drysalter ... 1707 ... A dealer in chemical products used in the arts, drugs, gums, etc; occas. also in oils, sauces, pickles, etc.' *Shorter OED.*

of seven or so. As a small or smallish girl she enjoyed history, metaphysics and biography, and among her favourite authors she included Fénélon and Blackstone—'mostly considered dry', she observed, 'by my companions'. Quakers of her day were notably liberal in their attitude to women, and her father, instead of being scandalised, as many of his non-Quaker contemporaries would have been, by Anna's intellectual force, gave her an excellent education. He also introduced her freely, along with his other children, to a wide circle of distinguished friends, including William Wordsworth and his brother Christopher (1774–1846), for 20 years Master of Trinity College Cambridge, whom Anna's elder sister Priscilla married. She cannot have been altogether a cosy young woman. 'Her mother Braithwaite is evidently quite afraid of her,' remarked Priscilla in 1810, 'and her husband is a model of obedience.'[19]

Isaac and Anna Braithwaite had seven sons and two daughters. Their eldest son, Isaac Braithwaite, was born in 1810 and lived until 1890. In 1833, under circumstances which we shall look at later, he became a partner in the firm which had been founded in 1825 as Foster & Janson. It then became Foster & Braithwaite and under that style, and with members of the Braithwaite family in it all the time, it has continued to the present day.

We are now in a position to see how the partnership of Foster & Janson, soon to become Foster & Braithwaite, fitted into the interwoven pattern of Quaker kinship and Quaker business which was its natural setting. The key figure, almost certainly, is Samuel Lloyd whose two nieces, the daughters of his brother-in-law and business associate Joseph Foster, were married to James Foster and Richard Janson.

At 57, in 1825, Samuel Lloyd wielded power and influence over a considerable field of business activity. In coal and iron he had been instrumental in bringing Lloyds Fosters into existence and two of his sons, along with two sons of Joseph Foster, were partners. In Taylors & Lloyds Bank, at Birmingham, his uncle Charles was senior to him, but he was 77 and infirm. Samuel was the managing partner.

Samuel must have been consulted when the firm of Foster & Janson was being set up. He may, indeed, have taken the initiative, or at least encouraged an initiative which was being taken. It would be extremely convenient for bankers in Birmingham and in other provincial towns to have a firm on the Stock Exchange whom they knew they could trust to do their business and the business of their customers. Equally for a new firm of stockbrokers it would be convenient to have a guaranteed source of commissions. What more reasonable, given the Quaker way of going about things, than for Samuel and others to encourage two young or youngish 'cousins' to set themselves up and then to see that they got enough orders to keep them going? At any rate, on '3rd day of 1st mo.' of 1825 James Foster and Richard Janson each drew £200 cash, and their firm was in business.[20]

REFERENCES

1 Humphrey Lloyd, *The Quaker Lloyds in the Industrial Revolution*, Hutchinson, 1975, pp. 276–277 and 165; typescript *Dictionary of Quaker Biography* at Friends' House, London.
2 Peter Mathias, *The Brewing Industry in England, 1700–1830*, CUP 1959, pp. 505–507.
3 As (1), p. 132.
4 As (2), p. 299.
5 L. S. Pressnell, *Country Banking in the Industrial Revolution*, Oxford (Clarendon), 1956, p. 242.
6 Lloyd, as (1), p. 59.
7 Estimated figures kindly supplied by the Society of Friends.
8 DQB; Percy Corder, *The Life of Robert Spence Watson*, Headley Brothers, London, 1914, pp. 18–19.
9 DQB.
10 Lloyd (as 1), pp. 218, 254–258, 276.
11 S. Lloyd, *The Lloyds of Birmingham*, pp. 199–201.

12 As (2), p. 294.
13 As (2), p. 288.
14 As (2), pp. 287–299; see also Lloyd (as 1), pp. 168, 170–171, 186, 192.
15 Lloyd (as 1), pp. 192, 218; Pedigree of Braithwaite of High Wray.
16 J. Bevan Braithwaite, *Memoirs of Anna Braithwaite*, Headley Brothers, London, 1905, p. 38.
17 T. I. Williams (ed.) *A Biographical Dictionary of Scientists*, A.&C. Black, 2nd Edn, 1974.
18 Lloyd (as 1), pp. 219, 232–233.
19 As (16), pp. 19, 26, 49, generally.
20 Private Ledger.

Chapter IV
The Patriarch, 1830–1880

On 21 June 1830—6 mo 21—the last transaction, a debit of a guinea, was recorded in Richard Janson's account with his firm. On 18 July he died, having presumably been ill not longer than three or four weeks. It was little enough warning for the death of a man three months to the day past his thirty-first birthday. He left a wife married two and a half years earlier, a son just over a year old, and James Foster as sole partner in the firm.[1]

Foster turned at once to the resources of the network of Quaker kin which we explored in Chapter III. Along at least two lines—one through his father and another through his wife—he was related to Isaac Braithwaite, drysalter of Kendal (p. ix above), and soon after Janson's death Foster asked Braithwaite to allow his eldest son, also Isaac, to go to London 'to make a trial of the business of stockbroker'. On 18 August 1830, just a month after Janson died, Isaac left Kendal and drysaltery for London and the Stock Exchange.

His mother was as pious as became a prominent Quaker minister:

8 mo 18th, 1830

Our beloved son Isaac, [she wrote in her private memoranda], left home for London. We keenly feel parting with him, and our prayers are put up for his preservation. May he continue clothed with the Divine fear and may he be a true disciple of our crucified Saviour.[2]

Concerned as she was for Isaac's spiritual welfare, she would hardly have been true to her Quaker upbringing if she had not looked to his worldly interests also, and Janson's death offered him an opportunity rare in 19th-century business: the opportunity to step into an established business without being closely related to the owner. Foster must have made it clear that if things went well Isaac would soon be offered a partnership, carrying with it an income that could already be expected to run comfortably into four figures: an attractive prospect for a youth still barely out of his teens, and no doubt very welcome to his parents. There were risks, of course, but Quakers were used to that.

Isaac had not long to wait. On 1 January 1833 his father's account in the private ledger was debited with £2,875 'to amount of Prem^m, on his son Isaac's becoming a partner'. The figure was arrived at in a rather arcane way. They took what appear to be profit figures for the years during which Isaac had been with the firm—1830, 1831, 1832—and added them together, giving £13,799 8s. 2d.* This sum they divided, more or less, by three, giving £4,600, and that they divided by four to give £1,150 which they multiplied by two and a half. With this sum Isaac Braithwaite, just short of his twenty-third birthday, was launched upon a partnership which was to last without a break, though with many alterations in its terms, until the end of 1888.

The firm altered its style from Foster & Janson to Foster & Braithwaite, but not immediately. For ten years or so the entry of Isaac, very much the junior partner, made no perceptible change in the general character of the business. From its earliest years the firm dealt in securities well outside the traditional and fairly safe market in British Funds.

* The arithmetic on which this sum is based is set out on a scrap of paper shut into the firm's first private ledger. The figures bear some relation, not very close, to Profit & Loss figures elsewhere in the same book.

In 1825, when it came into existence, the first recorded boom in company shares was roaring onward to disaster, and at the same time the riskiest kind of foreign loans were undeservedly—and briefly—popular. The firm's earliest books show sober Quaker names like Terry, Bevan, Fry and Forster, as well as many others, associated with far from sober speculation in Brazilian Mines, United Mexican Mines, Chile Mines, Royal Irish Mines. At home they were investing—prematurely—in the London & Birmingham Railway, the London & Bristol Railway, the London Northern Railway. In foreign loans, intoxicated apparently with the fashionable enthusiasm for liberalism, nationalism and colonial independence (outside British dominions), they took up Spanish Bonds, Portuguese Bonds, Chile Bonds, Colombian Bonds, and the notorious Greek Bonds of 1825.

These Greek bonds, launched by the Ricardos with a nominal value of £2 million at a price of 56½, eventually produced £275,000 or thereabouts for Greece, no interest for half a century for the investors, and a very nice return for those who promoted them.[3] In all these ways they were typical of a certain class of 19th-century foreign loans, of which we shall later have much more to say. Having survived the spectacular financial panic, particularly severe for country banks, which broke out late in 1825, Foster & Janson evidently settled to a steady round of the kind of business just described. On '2nd of 9th Mo 1833', still trading under the original style and describing themselves as 'British and Foreign STOCK BROKERS, and AGENTS for the Sale of CANAL, RAILWAY, SHARES &c.', they issued a share price list which happens to have survived. It shows shares and other securities associated with 64 canals; 11 docks, chiefly in London but including also Bristol, Folkestone and Shoreham; 27 insurance companies; 11 waterworks, in Birmingham, Liverpool, Manchester, Portsmouth and London; four bridges, all in London; 28 gas-light and coke companies widespread about the country, six London roads and a 'Thames Tunnel', presumably the one built by the two Brunels which to-day carries the underground line to New Cross; 14 railways, all at home; 16 mines, chiefly abroad; and 17 miscellaneous undertakings including General Steam Navigation and National Provincial Bank. They list also 'North American Funds', being chiefly the securities of the United States Government and of various states of the Union.

The firm's books, from the earliest times, show income under three main headings: 'Commission account', 'Continuation account' (after 1856 called 'Interest account') and 'General account'. The first heading refers to the ordinary business of a stockbroker, buying and selling on behalf of clients and charging commission for his services. 'Continuation', and later 'Interest', presumably covers income from speculative time bargains arranged for clients and from loans to clients. 'General Account', in sharp contrast to the other two, covers income from dealings not as brokers for clients but for the firm itself as principal.

Dealings on General Account, as time went on, were to become very important, but during the firm's first quarter-century—during the ascendancy, that is to say, of James Foster—they were usually negligible, although in 1835 income under the 'GA' head rose to 12 per cent of the total and in 1848 there was a loss equivalent to about 8 per cent of the firm's income for that year. Otherwise dealings on General Account never provided more than 3 per cent of total income and in several years there seem to have been no G.A. dealings at all.

Income from time bargains, arising as it did from speculation, varied widely. In some years it would provide a quarter or a third of the total, but when confidence was badly shaken, as in 1837–1878, it fell away to 4–5 per cent and took years to recover. Indeed it was never so buoyant as early on, in the years 1833 and 1834, when 35–37 per cent of income came from 'Continuation'.

The solid base of the business, in James Foster's time, rested on ordinary commission dealings. Up to 1850 they normally provided 80 per cent, more or less, of the firm's total income and in some years, particularly the bad ones, almost the whole of it.[4] This side of the business rested on a firm base of support from bankers, acting on their customers' behalf and their own. By the 1850s a permanent geographical pattern had begun to set. There was a London connexion, shown in the ledgers by the names of Glyn Mills, Mastermans, and Hanbury Taylor & Lloyd. In the provinces there were centres of strength in the North-West; in Yorkshire; in East Anglia, stretching over into the East Midlands; in Devon and Cornwall. Names which appear in the ledgers are the Manchester & Liverpool District Bank, the Bank of Liverpool, the Lancaster Bank in the North-West; the Knaresborough Bank in Yorkshire and the Chesterfield Bank; in East Anglia Alexander & Co. of Ipswich with five branches; in the South-West the Devon & Cornwall Banks—thirteen altogether—Tweedy Williams & Co. at Truro, Falmouth and Redruth, and T. & W. Bolitho. Day by day, the post brought orders in. Commission was shared and the business may not have been exciting, but it had the great merit of being reliable. Until the early 1840s there was no great growth. The total income of the firm reached nearly £10,000 in 1834 and 1835, in spite of a panic in the spring of the latter year, but it was usually a good deal less. In 1837 it fell to £3,170, nearly all commission business. Taxation was negligible and the accounts ignore it. Office expenses never ran so high as £600 and were frequently under £400 for the year. After providing for them, and for interest on capital, the partners were free to divide the remaining income between themselves and to provide for contingencies as they saw fit. In 1834 and 1835 they put altogether £7,260 in the contingency account, taking nothing for themselves in 1835, but in the next year they made up for this exemplary self-restraint by paying themselves £7,456 and putting nothing by. The articles of partnership have not come to light, but the figures show that until 1846 the profit was divided 2:1 in Foster's favour. The junior partner, how-ever, had little cause to complain. Apart from the year of voluntary restraint there were only two years—1837 and 1839—when he was entitled to less than £1,000, and fre-quently, especially in the early forties, his share was worth a good deal more.[5] His income represented, very solid middle-class comfort.

By 1840 Isaac evidently felt that his position was secure, for he married. His bride was Louisa Masterman, fifth child of John Masterman (1781–1862), banker of the City of London. Masterman was the grandson of a London coal merchant (1720–1770) and the son of a banker, William Masterman (1758–1845), who had apparently married a cousin, his wife being Lydia Mildred, daughter of Daniel Masterman (1759–1819). Here, evidently, was part of just such a family network of commerce and banking as the one to which Isaac himself belonged. It could hardly fail to bring business to Foster & Braithwaite.

The junior partner's father-in-law was a great man. His base was the family banking house of Masterman, Peters, Mildred, Masterman & Co. of 35 Nicholas Lane, but his influence ran far wider. He was an East India Director, a Deputy Lieutenant, one of the founders of the City of Lon-don Club. In 1841 he went into Parliament for the City as a Conservative 'prepared to resist any further con-cessions to popery',[6] and he held his seat until 1857.

As a banker he and his firm were much concerned with railway finance, being associated with other bankers and monied men and with the great contractors, Thomas Brassey (1805–1870) and Sir Samuel Morton Peto (1809–1889). By 1836 he was on the Board of the London & Southampton Railway, one of the most important of the early lines, built with the support of the War Office. The other Directors included a Liverpool banker, William Moss; William Chaplin, who had just sold the country's largest coaching business; and Matthew Uzielli of C. Devaux & Co., bankers and loan contractors. A contract for part of the line, from Basingstoke to Winchester, was let to Brassey.[7]

Masterman's association with Uzielli was lasting and, no doubt, lucrative. They were among the backers, in the early '40s, of the *Paris–Rouen–Le Havre* line and other lines in France and elsewhere. 'Masterman's leadership', wrote L. H. Jenks, 'was ubiquitous. He formed companies to seek concessions for the *Nord*, the *Paris–Lyons* and the *Orléans–Vierzon* routes. And while manœuvring for the ear of French deputies and bureau chiefs, the same capitalists organized the *Dutch–Rhenish* railway company which controlled for several years the only considerable line in Holland.'[8] About the same time, with other associates, he promoted another Brassey undertaking, the *Orléans–Bordeaux* line, and in the early '50s Masterman's name was linked with the *Paris–Lyons–Midi* line, in which Rothschilds and Barings had the major share, and with the *Ouest*.[9]*

Isaac Braithwaite's marriage to a girl so well connected, in the business sense, as Louisa Masterman must in any case have strengthened the position of his firm and his own position within it. In his particular case, it brought his firm into close contact with railway finance, at home and abroad, just at the beginning of a period of great opportunities and equally great risks. In the year of the marriage, 1840, railway affairs in Great Britain were passing through a phase of depression between the enthusiasm of the later 30s and the great construction boom of the mid-40s. New mileage authorised rose sluggishly from 15 in 1841 to 91 in 1843 and then shot up to 811 in 1844.[10] 'Projectors mapped out undertakings,' wrote D. Morier Evans in 1848, 'engineers patronised them, the schemes were advertised, and applications inundated the committees.'[11] What

---

* The authorities consulted leave doubt as to whether there were one, two, or three individuals of the name of Masterman concerned with all these undertakings. The style of the firm suggests there may have been two, probably father and son.

almost immediately came to be known as the 'Railway Mania' had begun.

It was at its height between Spring and Autumn, 1845, when the excitement over company promotion recalled, to those who remembered it, the excitement of 1825. 'Between the months of May and June', says Morier Evans, 'the increase of speculation was fearful. The papers teemed with advertisements.... Earls and Marquises struggled with London capitalists and rustic landowners to add attractiveness by the sanction of their names; the needy barrister professed affection for a seat at the councils of boards, which seemed likely to bring more profit than the law, and was ... importunate to be ensured that position.' Since no deposit was required with share applications, 'stagging'* was easy, costless and potentially very profitable: as Duguid much later observed, 'everyone who could write a presentable hand was welcome ... to ask for an allotment', and hundreds did so, though without the remotest intention—or the means—to take the allotment up. It seems to have been the first time that stags appeared in large numbers in the market, having no thought in their minds but to turn letters of allotment, if they got them, as soon as possible into cash. About 2,883 miles of new railway, in Great Britain and Ireland, were authorised in 1845—enough to double the existing system—and about 240 miles were opened.[12]

In August the Board of Trade doubled the deposit to be required from promoters of future railway bills from 5 per cent to 10 per cent of the capital proposed, and on 16th October Bank Rate went up from $2\frac{1}{2}$ per cent to 3. These two happenings between them produced first uneasiness and then panic, and share prices dropped as speculators scrambled out. £100 shares, £80 paid in the Great Western, one of the largest and soundest railways, touched

* A 'stag' applies for an allotment of shares not with any intention of taking them up but in the hope of selling them at a profit before he is called upon to pay for them.

£236 in August, dropped during October to £141, and finished the month at £154. The stock of another prominent railway, the London and North Western, dropped over the same period from £254 at the highest to £214 at the lowest, and finished at £220. 'The active progress of share gambling', commented Morier Evans three years later, '... received the first efficient check at this date.'[13]

The gamblers may have been checked, but not the projectors or the contractors. During 1846 nearly 4,800 miles of railway were authorised and about 440 opened. In 1847, a year of acute commercial crisis, the mileage authorised fell to about 1,600 miles and then tailed off rapidly, year by year, to only seven in 1850, after which it began to rise again.[14] The length of line opened, however, rose as the authorised schemes went ahead, and by the end of 1850 the mileage of railway open in Great Britain—about 6,000—was at least four times as great as ten years earlier.[15]

To build 4,500 miles of railway in ten years, almost entirely by hand, represented an explosive outburst of energy and optimistic self-confidence. The boom and panic of 1845, with its froth of fraudulent schemes and irresponsible 'stagging', subsided to leave an immense and fundamentally sound achievement: the main framework of the railway system of Victorian England, which itself was to carry the country forward to the vastly increased material prosperity of the latter part of the century, for the railway system was the indispensable foundation of a fully industrialised society.

The effect on the Stock Exchange of the building of the railways was to create something that had never existed before: a large market altogether independent of Government credit in any form, whether 'the Funds' or loans to foreign states. For the first time the small investor seeking safety could find a home for his (her) money in private enterprise, for the fixed interest securities of the larger home railways—the Great Western, the London & North Western, the Lancashire & Yorkshire, the North Eastern, for example—became virtually as solid as Consols. The wealthy capitalist, able to bear risks, could back new construction—especially, from the early '50s onward, in the United States. Throughout the field the knowledgeable speculator or the out-and-out gambler could play the market to his heart's content or his credit's limit.

As early as 1853 'Home Rails' represented nearly 16 per cent of the nominal value of all securities quoted on the London Stock Exchange, against 70 per cent represented by British Funds and nearly 6 per cent by foreign loans. As the mid-century years went by and railways spread across the world, colonial, American and foreign railways became important. By 1883 railway issues of all kinds represented over 40 per cent of the nominal value of quoted securities, against 24 per cent in British Funds and 23 per cent in foreign loans. Commercial and industrial issues, even in 1883, represented less than 7 per cent, but in the shape of railway stock and shares the finance of private enterprise had come to the market in a big way.[16]

Foster & Braithwaite, through their marriage alliance with Masterman's Bank, were well placed to share in the proceeds of this expanding market, and there is every indication that they did so. Moreover they evidently did so with judgement, for in the year 1845, when many stockbrokers went bankrupt (36 in 1845/6)[17], the firm's income was larger by far than it had ever been before. It rose spectacularly throughout the early '40s—the years when the railway boom was getting under way—from £4,183 in 1839, a bad year, to £50,649 in 1845. Of that sum James Foster took £24,000, Isaac Braithwaite £12,000, and £11,994 went for contingencies. Office expenses, at £2,056, were very high, but presumably that was the price of prosperity. Income fell sharply during the late '40s, but it picked up again in the early '50s, and in spite of fluctuations of as much as 75 per cent between one year and another (1845 and 1846) it is clear that in the years between 1840 and 1850 the firm's business became established permanently at a higher level than before.[18] Railways, as we shall shortly see, were important in its growth.

Either because of increased business or because Foster, in his sixties, was thinking of retirement, or perhaps for both reasons, the two partners decided, in the late 1840s, to bring in a third. Foster had no children and Braithwaite's sons were too young, and in that situation they might have been expected to bring in a more distant relation, but they did not, perhaps as a consequence of the bitter doctrinal quarrelling within the Society of Friends which in 1838 drove Isaac Braithwaite to the Church of England.[19] The new partner, Henry Waite, does not seem to have been related to either of them. He became a partner in 1848, with an agreement which allowed him $12\frac{1}{2}$ per cent of the profits. Foster and Braithwaite shared $87\frac{1}{2}$ per cent equally.[20] He spent the rest of his life with the firm.

J. N. F. Kellas, chief bookkeeper for many years, who came into the office in 1870, remembered Waite, in 1914, as 'a short, stout, fiery man. Very quick tempered and then very noisy and sometimes unreasonable. But then it was soon over and he would be quite nice again, speaking in a soft, low tone of voice and would apologise in some cases.' He became known in the City as 'the Royal Bengal Tiger', and in one of the few disputes which Foster & Braithwaite carried to the Stock Exchange Committee, against Lawrence & Cazenove in 1854, Waite was prominent. F&B won, but the Committee made it clear they thought the firm had been unwarrantably quarrelsome.[21]

James Foster retired from the firm and from the Stock Exchange on 30 June 1855. Among the generality of the membership he must have been well thought of, for he was elected to the Committee for General Purposes every year from 1838–1839 to 1852–1853. He stood again for 1853–1854, but polled too few votes to get in, and he did not try again. He died on 20 January 1861.[22] He spent thirty years as senior partner of Foster & Braithwaite, but there is no way of assessing his influence on the firm.

Dealings on General Account increased markedly after he retired, which suggests that his approach to his calling may have been more cautious than Isaac Braithwaite's: more than that we cannot say. No relations followed him, and his memory seems to have faded rapidly: we have no portrait of him either painted or written.

With Foster gone, Isaac Braithwaite, aged about forty-five and having twenty-five years' experience of the Stock Exchange, became head of the firm. We have no account of him as he was then. By the time Kellas knew him, he seems to have developed the style of a patriarch. He only came to the office once or twice a week and Kellas remembered him as 'a strict disciplinarian and very precise in everything'. Kellas once had occasion to report a clerk for deliberately delaying the closing of the books. The clerk later went into business on his own, 'caused a big loss to the Firm and ended his career by committing suicide': a *dénouement* which, Kellas considered, 'will shew how strong a deterrent an interview with Mr Braithwaite was'.[23]

Outside the business Braithwaite kept up the Quaker tradition, although no longer a Quaker, by taking an active part in religious affairs. He was not without influence, because he was first cousin, through his mother, to Christopher Wordsworth, Bishop of Lincoln from 1868 to 1885, and a close friend of Robert Bickersteth, Bishop of Ripon from 1857 to 1884. Both prelates were Low Churchmen and in the envenomed ecclesiastical politics of the day Isaac Braithwaite enthusiastically took the same side: as also, apparently, did his father-in-law (p. 39 above). Until the end of his life, it seems, he kept to the 'plain speech' of his Quaker boyhood. When his nephew Cecil Braithwaite, about 1879, did not know his way about the City, Uncle Isaac said: 'Go and find out, thou cannot learn younger.'[24]

The business of the firm, in Foster's later years and under Isaac, leant heavily towards the railway market. As early as the mid-'40s Foster & Braithwaite were brokers to various share issues at home, and it is safe to assume that the business came their way through Masterman's Bank, either directly or indirectly. In the early '50s, again in company with Mastermans, they began to look further afield: to the developing business in American railway finance.

North America, especially the USA, with its bounding economy and uninhibited freedom of capitalist enterprise, for many years offered an alluring prospect to the bolder spirits among railway investors and speculators. 2,800 miles of line had been built by 1840, chiefly in the Atlantic states but stretching inland also through Kentucky, Ohio, Indiana, Michigan and Illinois.

That mileage trebled by 1850 and trebled again in the '50s, as the lines were pushed over the Alleghenies towards the Great Lakes and as Illinois and other mid-Western states began to develop independent systems of their own, centring especially upon Chicago, which received its first locomotive, by sailing ship, in 1852. The Civil War, between 1861 and 1865, hardly checked the onward rush, which by then was beginning to be directed clean across the continent. The first transcontinental line was begun in 1862 and finished on 10 May 1869, and two more followed in the early '80s and the early '90s. During the '60s 20,000 miles of line were built; during the '70s, 40,000, and in the '80s lines were being laid at the rate of 7,000 miles a year.[25]

To finance this astonishing, long-sustained outburst of energy the Americans relied heavily on European, particularly British, investors.[26] In the earliest phase, during the '30s, a good deal of money went into railroads by way of State loans rather than direct issues by the railroad companies, but early in the '40s nine states defaulted, which turned that method of finance rather sour. At that time, in any case, British investors had plenty to keep them occupied in railways at home. On the Stock Exchange the market in American Rails, which Duguid says had been established by 1840, with about half-a-dozen jobbers, 'was absolutely wiped out'.[27]

'American Rails' began to revive in the early '50s. The securities then offered were not those of the discredited states but of the railroads themselves. They followed a pattern common in American company finance in the 19th century, in which equity capital representing—it was hoped—the earning power of the business supported a superstructure of fixed-interest bonds of greater or less, sometimes very much less, security. Many railroads issued mortgage bonds charged directly on their physical assets: track, buildings, cars and locomotives. To support other bonds, such as those issued in 1852 by the New York & Erie RR for which Foster & Braithwaite were brokers, trustees might be appointed to buy, out of the revenues of the line, 'United States Stocks, or other safe City or State Stocks'.[28] Any irony in this description was presumably unintentional. Railways in the Middle West, between 1850 and 1871, received grants of free land, amounting to 131 million acres (53 million hectares), which provided another credit base. Sterling bonds, paying a rather lower rate of interest, were issued, and so were bonds convertible, after a fixed period, into shares.

Not all railroads were the soundest of undertakings, and even where the general conception of a line was sound, the finances were sometimes shaky. Mortgages were piled on mortgages—by the New York & Erie, up to five times—and default and bankruptcy were common. Some lines, like the Philadelphia & Reading, made a habit of it. Harassed bondholders found themselves driven to form committees to protect their investments or even to take control. It was by no means uncommon for American railroads, more than usually embarrassed, to be run by remote control from London, and in the early 20th century Foster & Braithwaite had the unhappy experience of being on the London end of just such an episode (p. 122 below). On top of everything else, the railroads, with their potential

47

monopoly power, were the favourite battleground of some of the fiercest of the American 'robber barons'—Commodore Vanderbilt, Jay Gould, Jim Fiske, Edward H. Harriman, J. Pierpont Morgan—which not only put their finances at risk but also brought them into the centre of sharp political controversy.[29]

This was not a market for the innocent; for the cautious; for the small investor careful of his capital; nor even, it might be thought, for anyone sensitive to the finer points of business ethics. Nevertheless it was a market in which Foster & Braithwaite established a considerable reputation. In 1877 one of the partners appeared before a Royal Commission then sitting. 'You have a large business as brokers?' they said to him. 'Yes, certainly,' he replied, and when they asked 'What market is it chiefly in?' he answered: 'American principally.'[30]

The revival of British interest in 'American Rails' came in 1852 with the issue of a $5 million (£1 million) loan for the building of the Illinois Central RR. It was put out by Devaux & Co., Mastermans' associates, and it was gratifyingly successful: so much so that within a fortnight of its issue a prospectus was published of £500,000 debentures for the New York & Erie RR, carrying the names of Heywood Kennards as bankers and Foster & Braithwaite as brokers. About six months later, in January 1853, Foster & Braithwaite were brokers to a loan for the Chicago & Rock Island RR for which Mastermans were the bankers.[31]

Foster & Braithwaite may well have been in the American market before 1852. Certainly from that year onward until 1914 they remained very active in railway dealings, even after that section of the market lost some of its glamour in the '90s. The record of their dealings on General Account—on the firm's own behalf, that is, not for clients—exists in detail from 1857, and between that year and 1895 it lists 65 railroads in USA and ten in Canada, with the greatest activity in the '70s when, according to

Duguid, the American market was the busiest department of the Stock Exchange.[32]

They needed sound judgement and strong nerves. Writing in 1859, Morier Evans remarked on 'the prevalent belief'—in the United States—'that the chief lines were corruptly managed', and he went on to speak of 'the fearful indiscretion in the financial management of American railways'.[33] There is no reason to suppose that these faults improved as time went on: if anything they may have grown worse.

Markets in the USA and Europe were already heavily interdependent and Foster & Braithwaite had to steer their way through crisis after crisis, originating now on one side of the Atlantic, now on the other. In September 1854 they were writing to the bankers, Brown Shipley, of 'panic in the market for Railroad Bonds' in New York. It left bargains, no doubt, for those who survived with the resources to pick them up, but in Europe, as a series of letters to Brown Shipley shows, the uncertainties of the Crimean War kept stock markets disturbed and, on the whole, depressed until well into 1855 and probably later.[34]

In the Autumn of 1857 the failure of the Ohio Life & Trust Company set off a string of bank failures and other bankruptcies—over 5,000 in all, it was estimated—which contributed to a very severe commercial crisis, one of the worst of the century, in the United Kingdom in 1857–1858, and in the Spring of 1859 rumours of war in Europe caused a Stock Exchange panic, centring chiefly on The Funds, which fell to $88\frac{1}{4}$. It broke out over the Easter holidays, and between 21 and 29 April 1859 more than 50 firms were reported to have failed.[35] It would be unwise to rely too heavily on accounts written in the confusion of the moment, but they give a vivid impression of the prevailing mood. Foster & Braithwaite's income fell from £15,273 in 1858 to £9,312 in 1859 and they lost money on General Account: the message of these figures hardly needs underlining.[36]

'During the [American] Civil War [1861–65]', says Mrs Adler, 'new British investment in American railways virtually ceased.'[37] Foster & Braithwaite's activities on General Account, however, did not. They were doing some business in American rails throughout the conflict. Railways in the Confederate States, though, are conspicuously absent from the record, no doubt through deliberate policy.

On 'Black Friday', 11 May 1866, the failure of Overend, Gurney became known. They were an old, respected finance house in the City of London, and a great many other firms relied on them. Panic set in. 'No single bankruptcy', said *The Times* at the end of the year, has ever caused so great a shock to credit. Bank Rate went to 10 per cent, a rate only equalled, in the 19th century, in one other year: 1857.[38]

Foster & Braithwaite's business was shaken, though probably not on the American side. The crisis was brought on, according to Duguid, by heavy speculation in the shares of joint-stock banks between 1864 and 1866. Foster & Braithwaite, to judge from the evidence of the General Account, had played their full part in that. Between 1860 and 1865 they dealt in the shares of 18 banks, but they got out of them nearly all, it appears, before the crash and they were very wary indeed of bank shares for the rest of the century. The firm's income dropped from £44,654 in 1865 to £32,252 in 1866 and the income from General Account—usually, in these years, an indication of ebullience or the reverse—fell from 21 per cent of the larger total to 14 per cent of the smaller. In absolute figures, it halved, from £9,288 in 1865 to £4,515 in 1866.[39]

One of the casualties of 1866 was Masterman's Bank. In 1864, following a trend prevalent in banking at the time, it ceased to be a private bank and merged with the Agra and United Services Bank to form Agra & Masterman's Bank Limited. John Masterman had died in 1862 and no doubt the management had passed to a younger generation who may have thought his methods out of date. The initiative for the merger seems to have come from the Agra side. Most of that bank's shareholders and depositors were 'old military officers, civil servants and widows', and the management seems to have been seeking a more dashing image. In particular they wanted 'counter business' in London and they wanted to avoid paying commission to London agents, both of which objects might be achieved by marriage with Mastermans. Unfortunately the merger seems to have spoilt Agra's credit: the more so, no doubt, because the new bank began taking risky business in London and opened a branch in Paris, which *The Times* called 'their crowning error'. When the crisis came, a 'lying telegram' to Bombay, casting unjustified doubt on the soundness of the London end of the business, caused a run on branches throughout India. The London office could not help, the Bank of England would not, and Agra & Mastermans stopped payment. *The Times* thought the failure 'a calamity which will inflict far greater suffering than any event which has yet taken place since the commencement of the crisis'.[40] There is no evidence that it was especially serious for Foster & Braithwaite, although they held shares, but it presumably destroyed any value there may still have been in the Masterman connection.

In line with the general tendency of the market and the increasing pace of railroad construction, Foster & Braithwaite's business in 'American rails' rose to a peak in the '70s. From 1880 onward it began to take a different course, but that we shall examine in its place. The '70s produced some excellent results for Foster & Braithwaite, with the firm's income, in the best years, running at levels which were not attained again for a good many years, but it was a difficult decade in a difficult market.

To start with, between 1868 and 1872 a furious and exceptionally corrupt war was fought for the control of the New York & Erie RR. The corruption was not all-American. The English stockholders, who were numerous and powerful, eventually got rid of their principal adversary, Jay Gould, with the aid of a fund of $300,000 with which they persuaded directors appointed by Gould to resign.[41] On the Stock Exchange, the leaders of the fight against Gould were Tom Nickalls (the 'Erie King') and Edward Satterthwaite[42] and there is no evidence that Foster & Braithwaite were particularly prominent, though they must have been closely interested. They had been associated with an issue of Erie bonds in 1852 (p. 48) and throughout the '60s and '70s they were dealing in various classes of Erie securities on General Account.

Charles Branch, Foster & Braithwaite's American expert from 1863 to 1877, summed up the firm's experience in the mid-'70s in evidence to the Royal Commission of 1877. In 1873, he said, there was a panic in railroad stocks and they were 'very much shaken'. After that 'an enormous speculation was begun in them, and it was supposed to have been planned (I think there is no doubt about it) by an organised gang'. They employed two brokers, one to buy and the other to sell. They forced prices down and then bought in again.[43] It was a device of a kind very familiar on the Victorian Stock Exchange: part of the apparatus of market-rigging which critics of the Stock Exchange repeatedly and justifiably seized upon and which its defenders regarded with a good deal of complacency.[44]

Branch was closely concerned with Foster & Braithwaite's American business during most of the hectic—but profitable—'60s and '70s. When he gave evidence to the Royal Commission he had just retired after, he said, 27 years 'man and boy' as a stockbroker. He was evidently interpreting that description liberally, for he did not become an unauthorised clerk*—with Foster & Braithwaite—until 1854. He was 'authorised' a year later, became a member in 1861, and a partner in 1863.[45] When Kellas joined in 1870 he found Branch 'an authority on "Americans"'. He told the Royal Commission that his business

* 'Stockbrokers' clerks may be 'authorised' to deal on behalf of their firms, or 'unauthorised'.

had 'consisted largely of operations in American securities' and had compelled him 'to deal extensively in the American markets, especially at New York and Philadelphia'. He dealt, he said, through agents, but Cecil Braithwaite's memoirs suggest that he crossed the Atlantic at least once.

In Branch's time there were probably not many firms classed alongside Foster & Braithwaite as American specialists. E. F. Satterthwaite's firm, which went bankrupt in 1894 and was barred from the Stock Exchange for pledging clients' securities[46] was one, and another was Heseltine & Powell. They had offices opposite Foster & Braithwaite, and Branch and Heseltine, according to Kellas 'were inseparables in the American market'.

Foster & Braithwaite, and possibly Heseltines, acted as 'jobbing brokers', combining two functions which by the custom of the Stock Exchange were traditionally kept separate.[47] J. H. Daniell, Government broker and 'accepted head of the Stock Exchange',[48] suggested to the Royal Commission of 1877 that 'a man very much concerned in American securities, some of which no one knew anything about but himself, might be a jobber in those particular securities, and yet ... a broker for all other purposes.'[49] That, no doubt, was Foster & Braithwaite's position, but there may have been more to it than that. Branch himself did not like jobbers and was very jealous of the 'jobber's turn'. 'It takes a lifetime,' he told the Royal Commission, 'for a broker to get together a connexion and to keep it ... it needs ... an expensive establishment of clerks, expensive offices near the Stock Exchange, and other necessary considerable outlays.' For that, he said, all he got was a commission of $\frac{1}{2}$ per cent or $\frac{1}{4}$ per cent if he had to split it with a bank. The jobber, on the other hand, 'with no necessary outgoings except his subscription to the Stock Exchange, with positively a book and a pencil for his stock in trade, makes ... two, three, four, or five times the commission which I receive. Now I say that is a weakness and blot upon the system.'[50]

Naturally the jobbers did not like Branch very much, nor Heseltine either. Kellas tells a story, dating presumably from the '70s, of Branch and Heseltine being surrounded in the House by a ring of jobbers singing a song called 'The Conspirators' Chorus' from a light opera of the day. In the end the jobbers won. In 1877—the year when Branch retired—the Stock Exchange Committee objected to Foster & Braithwaite's jobbing activities and they gave them up.[51]

Apart from any speculation they may have indulged in, Foster & Braithwaite were interested in a rather rarefied form of activity for a London stockbroker: the marketing of American railroad bonds. Between 1852 and 1876 they were associated with at least seven issues:[*]

1852 £500,000	New York & Erie 6 per cent sterling debentures: no issue price in the prospectus (!)	
1853 $400,000	Chicago & Rock Island bonds[†] at £200 for a $1,000 bond	
1867 £200,000	Pennsylvania 6 per cent general mortgage sterling bonds at 82	
1873 £200,000	Baltimore & Ohio 6 per cent sterling debentures at $99\frac{1}{2}$	
1874 £2,000,000	Pennsylvania 6 per cent consolidated sterling bonds at 90 (second *tranche* of an issue made, without F&B., in 1873)	
1875 $3,000,000	Central of New Jersey 7 per cent currency bonds at 95	
1876 £600,000	Pennsylvania 6 per cent consolidated mortgage sterling bonds at 90.	

† coupon not stated

* This list is made from Adler, pp. 62, 96 and Appendix I (American Railway Securities Issued Publicly in London 1865–1880), and from Kellas's reference, in his reminiscences, to 'Central of New Jersey 5%'. This is presumably the 1875 issue listed by Mrs Adler, but she does not connect F&B with it, only Brown Shipley, and she quotes a 7 per cent coupon.

PRICES OF SHARES

BY

FOSTER & JANSON,

BRITISH AND FOREIGN STOCK BROKERS, AND AGENTS FOR THE SALE OF CANAL, RAILWAY, SHARES, &c.

64, OLD BROAD STREET.

LONDON, 1st of 5th Mo. 1833.

No. Shares	CANALS.	Price per Share	Div. per Share per Ann.	Dividends Due.
1760	Ashton and Oldham, Average 97l 18s sh	125 ..	£5 ..	September
1482	Ashby-de-la-Zouch .... Average 113l sh	74 ..	4 ..	
720	Barnsley .... 160l sh	290 ..	14 ..	1Jan. 1July
1260	Basingstoke .... 100l sh	5½..	.. ..	
1005	Brecknock and Abergavenny .. 150l sh	80 ..	5 ..	1Jan. 1July
4000 ⅛ sh.	Birmingham ⅛ share 17l 10s	238 ..	12 10	1 Ap. 1 Oct.
4000	Birmingm & Liverpl Juncn 100l sh. all pd	38 a 39	.. ..	
477	Bolton and Bury .... 250l sh	105 ..	6 ..	Jan.
600	Bridgewater and Taunton .... 100l sh	70 ..	.. ..	
400	Chelmer and Blackwater .... 100l sh	102 ..	5 ..	Jan.
500	Coventry .... 100l sh	.. ..	32 ..	May Nov.
460	Cromford .... 100l sh	.. ..	17 ..	
4546	Croydon .... Average 31l 2s 10d sh	.. ..	.. ..	
11,810l.	Ditto....Bonds....various amounts ..	.. ..	5 per c.	
600	Derby .... 100l sh	120 ..	6 ..	Jan. July
2060¾	Dudley .... 100l sh	43 ..	2 10	Mar. Sept.
3575½	Ellesmere and Chester, Average 133l sh	76½..	3 15	1 Sept.
231	Erewash .... 100l sh	800 ..	52 ..	
1297	Forth and Clyde .. Average 400l 16s sh	545 a 550	27 ..	Jan. July
11,550	Grand Junction .... 100l sh	230 a 231	12 ..	June Dec.
2849⅜	Grand Union .... 100l sh	23½..	1 ..	Oct.
19,327l.	Ditto (Loan Notes) various amounts ..	.. ..	5 per c.	Mar. Sept.
1521	Grand Surrey .... 100l sh	.. ..	.. ..	Mar. Sept.
120,000	Ditto (optional) Loan .... 100l sh	85 a 87½	5 per c.	June Dec.
3096	Grand Western .... 100l sh 94l pd	.. ..	.. ..	
600	Glamorganshire, Average cost 172l 13s 4d	290 ..	13l 12s 8d	Mar. June
1960	Gloucester and Berkeley .... 100l sh	14 ..	.. ..	Sept. & Dec.
269	Ditto (optional) Notes 60l	102 ..	5 per c.	
749	Grantham .... 150l sh	202 ..	10 ..	May
6238	Huddersfield .... Average 57l 6s 6d sh	30 ..	1 ..	1 Sept.
25,328	Kennet & Avon .. Average 39l 18s 10d sh	28 ..	1 5	1 Sept.
11,699½	Lancaster .... Average 47l 6s 8d sh	25 ..	1 ..	5 April
2897¾	Leeds and Liverpool .... 100l sh	455 a 460	£20 ..	1May 1Nov.
546	Leicester .... 140l sh	185 ..	12 ..	1Jan. 1July
1907	Leicester and Northampton, Av. 83l 10s	89 ..	4 ..	June Dec.
70	Loughborough .... Average 142l 17s sh	1850	144 ..	Jan. July
3000	Macclesfield .... 100l sh	.. ..		
2409	Monmouthshire .... 100l sh	.. ..	10 ..	June Dec.
700	Montgomeryshire .... 100l sh	85 ..	4 ..	August
250	Melton Mowbray .... 100l sh	190 ..	9 ..	July
500	Mersey and Irwell .... 100l sh	720 ..	40 ..	June
247	Neath .... 100l sh	.. ..	18 ..	July
522	Oakham .... 130l sh	39 ..	2 ..	
1786	Oxford .... 100l sh	570 ..	32 ..	Mar. Sept.
2400	Peak Forest .... Average about 78l sh	75 ..	3 ..	24Ju. 24Dc.
2520	Portsmouth and Arundel .... 50l sh	15 ..	.. ..	
21,418	Regent's .... Average 33l 16s 8d sh	16½..	13 6	July
5669	Rochdale .... Average 85l sh	95 ..	4 ..	April
500	Shropshire .... 125l sh	134 ..	7 10	June Dec.
800	Somerset Coal .... 150l sh	170 ..	10 10	30Ju. 30Dc.
45,000	Ditto Lock Fund Stock .... 12l 10s sh	12½..	5½ p.c.	30Ju. 30Dc.
700	Stafford and Worcester .... 140l sh	555 ..	32 ..	Feb. Aug.
500	Shrewsbury .... 125l sh	255 ..	11 ..	May Nov.
300	Stourbridge .... 145l sh	196 ..	8 ..	Jan. July
3647	Stratford-on-Avon .... Av. 79l 9s 8d sh	33¾ .	1 5	Oct.
200	Stroudwater .... 150l sh	510 ..	23 ..	May Nov.
533	Swansea .... 100l sh	.. ..	11 ..	Nov.
1300	Thames and Severn, black .... 100l sh	25 ..	£1 10	5 June
1150	Do....Do....red .... 100l sh	29 ..	£1 10	5 June
2600 ½ sh.	Trent and Mersey, ½ sh. 100l	660 ..	37 10	June Dec.
350	Tavistock (Mineral) .... 100l sh	.. ..	2 ..	
4805	Thames and Medway .. Ave. 30l 4s 3d sh	15s ..	.. ..	
3344	Thames and Medway, New Shares, 3½ sh. 3l. pd.	.. ..		
1000 sh. & 1000 ½	Warwick and Birmingham .... 100l sh	280 ex.d.	15 ..	Mar. Sept.
980	Warwick and Napton .... 100l sh	220 ex.d.	12 ..	May Nov.
6000	Worcester and Birmingham, Av. 78l 8s sh	87 ..	3 10	Feb.
20,000	Wilts and Berks .. Average 16l 17s 8d sh	4½..	.. 5s	May 31
800	Wyrley and Essington .... 125l sh	115 ..	6 ..	
126	Wisbeach .... 105l sh	45 ..	.. ..	May
905	Way and Arun .... 110l sh	22½..	1 ..	May

No. Shares	DOCKS.	Price per Share.	Div. per Share per Ann.	Dividends due.
2209	Bristol .... Average 147l 9s sh	.. ..	£3 6 4	Dec. 2.
68,324l.	Ditto Notes	.. ..	5 per c.	May Nov.
2600 & 1065½ sh.	Commercial .... 100l sh	70 ..	4 ..	Jan. July
16,000	Ditto Bonds .... 100l ..	55 ..	4 per c.	Jan. July
483,750	East India .... Stock ..	49 ..	4 per c.	Mar. Sept.
1038	East Country .... 100l sh	7 ..	.. ..	
570	Folkestone Harbour .... 50l sh	4 ..		
ab. 15,000	Ditto Bonds, various amounts		5 per c.	
3,238,310l. 5s. 10d.	London .... Stock ..	58 ..	3 per c.	June Dec.
	Shoreham Harbour	.. ..	10	Jan. 1831.
7500	South London .... 100l sh. 3l pd	.. ..	4 p. c.	Apr. Oct.
1,352,752	St. Katherine's .... Stock ..	68 ..	3 p. c.	Jan. July
500,000	St. Katherine's Dock Bonds	.. ..	4½ p. c.	5 Ap. 5 Oct.
200,000	Ditto ditto for 10 years ..	102½..	4 p. c.	Do.
1,380,000l.	West India .... Stock ..	88 ..	5 per c.	June Dec.
	INSURANCE COMPANIES			
2000	Albion .... 500l sh. 50l pd	73 ..	£3 10	Dec.
50,000	Alliance .... 100l sh. 10l pd	10 a 10½	4 p. cent	April
50,000	Ditto Marine .... 100l sh. 5l pd	4¾ a 5	5 p. cent	
24,000	Atlas .... 50l sh. 5l pd	10¾..	10s.	July
1200 ¼ sh.	Birmingham Fire .... 250l 55l pd	96 ..	£4	1 May
20,000	British .... 250l sh. 50l pd	35½..	4 p. c.	Mar. Sept.
12,000	British Commercial .... 50l sh. 5l pd	5¾..	5½ p. c.	Jan. July
5000	Cler. Med. & Gen. Life, 100l sh. 2l 10s pd	3½..	4 p. c.	
4000	County Fire .... 100l sh. 10l pd	40 ..	2 10	Dec.
30,000	Crown Life .... 50l sh. 5l pd	.. ..		
40,000	Eagle .... 50l sh. 5l pd	5¼..	5s	Oct.
200	Economic Life .... 1000l sh. 250l pd	300 ..	5½ ..	Jan. July
2271	European Life .... 20l sh	21 16	5½ ..	Jan. July
50,000	Ditto ditto New .... 20l sh. 2l pd	1⅜..	2s.	Jan. July
1,000,000l.	Globe .... Stock	150 ..	7 per c.	Jan. July
20,000	Guardian .... 100l sh. 20l pd	28 ..	1 ..	July
40,000	Hope .... 50l sh. 5l pd	6½ a ¾	Fire 5 p.c. Life 8 p.c.	May Nov.
2400	Imperial Fire .... 500l sh. 50l pd	104 ..	5 5	June Dec.
7500	Imperial Life .... 100l sh. 10l pd	9 ..	9s.	June
2020	Kent Fire .... 50l sh	66 ..	3 0	Sept.
10,000	Law Life .... 100l sh. 10l pd	17½..	....	
3900	London Fire .... 25l sh. 12l 10s pd	23 ..	1 ..	Mar. Sept.
31,000	London Ship .... 25l sh. 12l 10s pd	23 ..	1 ..	Mar. Sept.
40,000	Palladium .... 50l sh. 2l pd	2 ..	5 p. c.	Feb. Aug.
250,000	Protector Fire .... 20l sh. 2l pd	1 7 6	1s 6d	15 June
2500	Provident Life .... 100l sh. 10l pd	18½..	£1	July
100,000	Rock Life .... 20l sh. 2l pd	4 4	3s.	Aug.
689,219l. 17s. 10d.	Royal Exchange .... Stock ..	180 ..	5 pr. c.	Jan. July
1500	Union .... 200l sh. 20l pd	55 ..	10½ p.c.	Jan. July
	WATER WORKS.			
4800	Birmingham .... 25l sh. 24l pd	19 a ½		
4433 2-6th	East London .... 100l sh	120 ..	5 ..	Sept. Mar.
4500	Grand Junction .. Average 41l 13s 4d sh	57 a 58	2 10	Jan. July
2000	Kent .... 100l sh	39½..	2 0	Jan. July
388	Liverpool Bootle .... 220l sh	300 ..	8 ..	1 Aug.
6486	Manchester and Salford .... 100l sh	45½..	1 ..	January
1500	New River London Bridge Water Ann.	11½ pm.	2 10	Apr. Oct.
1500	Portsmouth and Farlington .... 50l sh	4 ..	....	
390	Ditto (new) .... 50l sh	33 ..	2 0	Mar.
800	South London .... 100 sh	78 ..	4 ..	5 Ap. 5 Oct.
8300	West Middlesex .... Average 63l 12s 9d	75½..	3 ..	Ju. 10. De. 10
1360	York Buildings .... 100l sh	34 ..	1 14	Ap. Oct.
	BRIDGES.			
1600	Hammersmith .... 50l sh	20 ..	1 ..	Jan. July
7231	Southwark .... Average 63l 2s 8d	2¾..	....	
1700	Ditto (new) .... 50l sh	20 ..	1 15	Dec.
5000	Waterloo .... 100l sh	2½..	....	
5000	Ditto Old Ann. of 8l per ann... 60l pd	23½..	1l 2s 0d	23 Fb. 23 Ag.
5000	Ditto New ditto of 7l.. " .... 40l pd	20½..	19s 3d	23 Fb. 23 Ag.
60,000	Ditto (Bonds) .... various amounts	113 ..	5 pr. c.	23 Fb. 23 Ag.
6000	Vauxhall .... Average 70l 10s 3d sh	18½..	1 ..	Jan. July

1 Share Price List issued by Foster & Janson, 1833, long before limited liability became widespread. See pp. 36–37.

2 An extract from Foster & Janson's Day Journal showing business done between 27 February and 1 March 1828

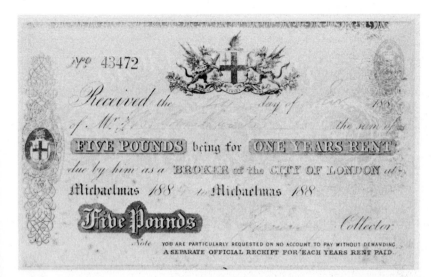

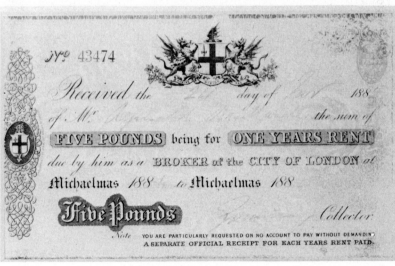

3 From time immemorial until 1884, stockbrokers to their great irritation were nominally under the authority of the City Corporation, from whom they were obliged to take out licences of which two specimens are illustrated. See pp. 10–11.

J.B.BRAITHWAITE

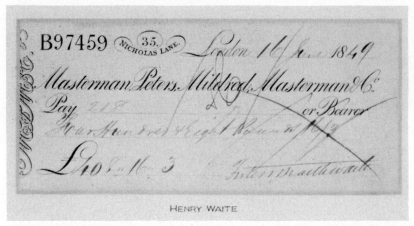

HENRY WAITE

4 Cheques drawn by the firm or by partners on banks with which Foster &
Braithwaite had dealings in the 19th century, including one from Masterman's
Bank in which Isaac Braithwaite's father-in-law was a partner.

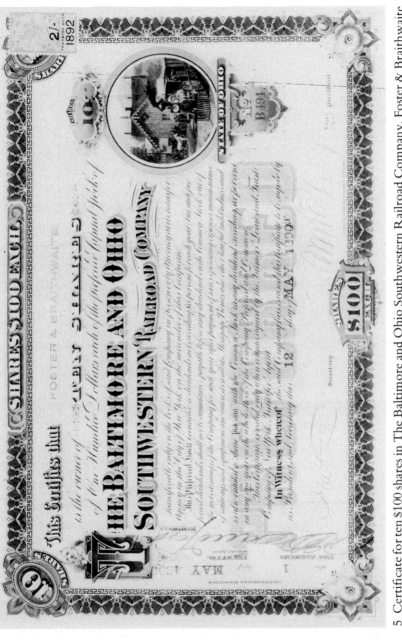

5 Certificate for ten $100 shares in The Baltimore and Ohio Southwestern Railroad Company. Foster & Braithwaite were specialising in American railroad securities at least as early as 1852. See Chapters IV and VI.

6 City characters, June 1882.

7 A sketch from *The Illustrated London News* of 1859 of Comayagua, the capital of Honduras. For the shocking story of the Honduras loans of 1867, 1868, 1870 and 1872, see pp. 70–79.

We know nothing of the internal mechanics of these issues: neither the terms on which Foster & Braithwaite agreed to act, nor the precise services they were required to render. On the analogy of other Victorian loans they would have been expected, as brokers to the issues, to get an official quotation and to carry out any of the manœuvres necessary for 'making a market' in order to do so.

Stockbrokers rarely acted independently in these matters, and F&B's issues were all made in association with other firms, chiefly bankers and a finance company, but including also Heseltine & Powell. For the Erie issue of 1852 Foster & Braithwaite's associates were the bankers Heywood Kennard, whose name appears in the prospectus, and Brown Shipley as trustees. Rothschilds were said to be interested but they rarely, if ever, allowed their name to be publicly associated with American railroad bonds, so that no blame could be attached to them for default.[52] Mastermans, less coy, appeared as Foster & Braithwaite's associates in the Chicago & Rock Island issue of 1854.

In two of the later issues—Pennsylvania Bonds of 1867 and 1874—Foster & Braithwaite's associates were the London, Asiatic & American Company, a finance house in which F&B held shares. It had been formed by merging three firms with interests in India and America, and it came into existence during the mid-'60s, on a wave of company promotion which followed new legislation on limited liability. Companies for many purposes were formed at that time, but finance companies and joint-stock banks (p. 50 above) were particularly fashionable.[53] Kellas says that J. S. Morgan & Co., very prominent indeed as promoters of railroad issues, were also associated with one of the Pennsylvania issues, probably the one in 1874. In two other issues, for Baltimore & Ohio in 1873 and for Pennsylvania in 1876, Foster & Braithwaite's only associates, publicly announced, were Heseltine & Powell, but there may have been financiers behind the scenes—the firm's folklore has it that there was at one time a close link with Rothschilds.

No separate account dealing with bond issues has survived, so we cannot be certain how profitable they were. It seems reasonably safe to assume, however, that the proceeds will have been brought into the General Account. Bearing that assumption in mind, we find that in the years when bond issues were made the income figures show the following pattern:

	Total Income	Income from General Account	
	£	£	% of total
1852	53,664	11,332	21
1853	37,651	12,539	33
1867	23,873	8,079	34
1873	73,669	51,677	70
1874	79,263	54,580	69
1875	66,806	24,201	36
1876	47,598	28,776	78

1867 was a bad year, and it looks as if General Account income saved it from being even worse, because it was nearly twice as great as in 1866 whereas commission income was 39 per cent down and 'interest' almost 50 per cent. 1876 was not very good, either, and once again General Account came to the rescue. Otherwise the years of bond issues were all good and two—1852 and 1874—were outstandingly good. In all these years, particularly two of the best—1873 and 1874—General Account contributed heavily to the total, suggesting that bond issues were usually highly profitable. Kellas, nevertheless, speaks of an issue for the Baltimore & Ohio—presumably the one in 1873, unless there was one of which we have no record—as 'disastrous', and he says that Central of New Jersey 5 per cent, by which he may have meant the 7 per cent issue of 1875, 'was a very bad issue for us', so it is necessary to look at these figures with caution.

There is no doubt of the success of various operations in Pennsylvania RR 6 per cent consolidated sterling bonds issued in 1873 and 1874. 2 million were issued, apparently in two '*tranches*'. The first, in 1873, was brought out by London, Asiatic & American on their own; the second, in 1874, by LAA, Foster & Braithwaite, and Heseltine & Powell jointly. A letter, dated 16 September 1874, from LAA to Foster & Braithwaite has survived. Its contents imply that the two issues were treated as one and that Foster & Braithwaite shared in the profits of both by way of a pool of £700,000 Bonds, later reduced to £584,000, of which the firm was allowed to take up a proportion at 85 against an issue price of 90. With their letter LAA sent a cheque for £17,995 17s 8d, representing Foster & Braithwaite's share of the pool profits. Kellas, presumably referring to this issue (he gives no dates), says that it was 'very successful ... our share of the profit being over £7,000'. Presumably Foster & Braithwaite had subdivided the firm's interest in the pool.

'American Rails', though predominant, were not the whole of Foster & Braithwaite's business during the third quarter of the 19th century. They did a little business in foreign and colonial railway securities and kept up a steady interest in railways at home, dealing with the securities of nearly 60 companies on General Account between 1857 and the early '80s. Their other activities spread over banking, finance, insurance, property, public utilities, shipping, telegraphs, mining, and ten companies classifiable only as miscellaneous commercial and industrial. The Funds they did not deal in, on General Account, but they dealt widely in the stocks of foreign countries, including some very risky ones, and in the stocks of American states and British Dominions and colonies, including some municipal stocks in USA and Canada.[54]

Kellas says that in his early days the firm was doing 'a

very large Contango business in the "House" and had as much as £400,000, or more, on Loan, from one Bank', but he does not go into details beyond saying, 'Contangoes would total between £8,000 and £9,000 a month,' and there is no way now of reconstructing this side of the business. It is not even certain how it was accounted for in the partners' ledgers, though probably under the heading 'Interest'. If that is so, there was no income at all from contangoes in 1873 and 1876 to 1878, which is very surprising. During most years of the third quarter of the century income under the 'Interest' heading ran between 20 per cent and 30 per cent of the total, occasionally dropping below 20 and in 1865 rising to 34 per cent, but when it began again after the hiatus in the late '70s it was much more irregular and generally at a lower level.[55]

The firm's connexion with banks, during this period, was growing and changing with the development of the banking system as a whole. There were still many independent banks—the firm's ledgers for 1872 to 1875 show thirty or more names—but limited liability and chains of branches are much more conspicuous than earlier. In the North, Foster & Braithwaite were dealing with the head office and ten branches of the York City & County Bank and with the head office and five branches of the York Union. In East Anglia and districts near it they did business with the Stamford Spalding & Boston Bank in all those towns and in nine others. Their ledger entries for the Devon & Cornwall Banks show seventeen branches.

The banks shared the firm's commission, and the firm did not like that. Alfred, Isaac Braithwaite's eldest son, complained to the Royal Commission about it. 'I do not see,' he said, 'why brokers should work for the advantage of bankers or any other profession,' adding plaintively: 'I do like a small quid for my quo, but they give me nothing.' The Commissioners were unsympathetic. 'Is it not a fact with you,' one of them asked, 'that the bankers' business comes to you regularly every morning, either by post or in the city as a lump as it were?' Alfred had to agree, but, he insisted, 'this is the only advantage that banking business gives us, but this I maintain is not nearly sufficient equivalent or justification for exacting the half commission.'[56] It is perhaps fair comment that the bankers provided a safety net for the firm to fall back upon when more exciting business—American bonds, perhaps—was lacking or went wrong.

Kellas draws a vivid and endearing picture of Alfred, by this time a partner: of Alfred 'balancing himself on the top of the fender' while he ate bread-and-milk for lunch; of Alfred, referring to his own speculations, saying: 'Turn to the disastrous account'; of Alfred saying: 'Such a nuisance it is having to wear clothes in this hot weather, let's all come down naked to-morrow, I will if you will!' He used to practise revolver shooting in the basement of the office until, growing bolder, he installed a cannon. 'On the last occasion on which it was fired there was crammed into it an excessive charge and it was put under the table. Mr Alfred ran out, shutting in Mr Jones. A large piece near the muzzle of the gun was blown out and the drawers in the bottom of the table splintered. Mr Jones was none the worse. Both the perpetrators considered it a huge joke.' Kellas was very fond of Alfred, who became a partner in 1866 when he was twenty-three, but he says nothing of Alfred's business ability.

Albert Leland Noel came into the partnership in 1860 as a direct result of Isaac Braithwaite's religious enthusiasm. He was the son of the Rev. Baptist Wriothesley Noel (1798–1873), a Scottish evangelical clergyman of considerable reputation whom Isaac greatly admired. In 1849 he took the remarkable step of joining the Baptists, and in 1855 and 1867 he was President of the Baptist Union.[57] Kellas calls A. L. Noel 'a thorough aristocrat' (his grandfather was a baronet) though radical in his politics, and he may have had bookish tastes for he chose to have himself photographed seated, book in hand, in a pose more like that of a don than of a stockbroker. Kellas says he was popular in the office but does not indicate what contribution he made to the business.

Another of Isaac Braithwaite's sons, Reginald, became a partner, aged twenty-six, in 1873. Kellas calls him 'quite a gay young man—not in the office, but outside', fond of driving four-in-hand. He had moved, it seems, some way from his father's affluent but plain Quaker background. Later on he developed an enthusiasm for the Church Army.

The partnership, then, steadily increased—a measure, no doubt, of the size and prosperity of the firm's business—from two to three in 1860, from three to four in 1863, from four to five in 1866, and to six when 'Reggie' came in in 1873. If Kellas is a reliable witness, it seems probable that when he joined the main weight of the business was being carried by Henry Waite, Charles Branch, and possibly A. L. Noel. The partners' rewards were considerable. In 1874, a good year, Isaac Braithwaite's share of the total income was £15,000 (in 1873, £20,000); Henry Waite's was £12,000; Noel, Branch and Alfred Braithwaite had £6,000 each; and Reggie, the junior partner in his second year, had £3,000. All the partners had ample opportunity for adding to their incomes—or not, as the case might be—by speculation. At a time when £500 a year would support an establishment of cook, housemaid and foot-boy,[58] the partners in Foster & Braithwaite were very comfortably off.

Neither Waite nor Noel nor Branch was related in any way, so far as we can tell, to Foster or to Braithwaite. To have so many unrelated partners was in a sense a temporary arrangement, bridging the gap in the succession caused by Foster's childlessness and the youthfulness of Isaac Braithwaite's sons, which made it impossible to bring them in when additional partners first began to be needed. It did not mean that Isaac Braithwaite, when he became head of the firm after Foster retired, had any intention at all of letting the partnership slip permanently out of the hands of his family and their close relations. On the contrary, he meant to establish the hereditary principle in Foster & Braithwaite's business firmly, narrowly and permanently, and by 1867 he was in a position to do so.

In 1867 a new deed of partnership was drawn up. Basing itself on Isaac Braithwaite's ownership of most of the capital employed in the business, it established his absolute sovereignty over it. The capital was held to consist of 48 shares of £1,000 each. 28 shares belonged to Isaac, to be held by him alone or by him and one or more of his sons or nominees. 12 shares belonged to Waite and four each to Noel and Branch. Thus entrenched, Isaac's powers were very wide. He had unrestricted rights to nominate partners and get rid of them. He could take over the shares of outgoing partners, or partners who died. He was entitled to say how the business should be run and to determine disputes arising among the other partners. The partners were required to employ themselves 'diligently and faithfully' in the business 'at all necessary and proper times' but it was specifically provided 'that it shall not be incumbent on the said Isaac Braithwaite to devote more of his time and attention to the business than he shall himself in his sole discretion from time think expedient or desirable'.

Isaac, at 57, was thinking of retirement and of the succession to the partnership, especially after his death. To signal the privileged position of his immediate family, an early clause in the deed—clause five—provided in effect, though not in so many words, that the names of any of Isaac's sons who were or should become partners should always stand, in the list of partners, ahead of all others except Henry Waite.

The deed went on to confer the right of nominating new partners on Isaac Braithwaite himself, on 'successors' to be nominated by him, and thereafter on a self-perpetuating line of successors. They would all be partners in the firm, there would be no more than four of them at a time, and each would be qualified by the ownership of not less than six forty-eighths of the firm's capital. Isaac was absolutely free in his choice of new partners: not so his successors. They were required to exercise their powers of nomination in favour of descendants of Isaac's father and, furthermore, each was to make his choice from among his own sons, brothers, nephews or descendants in these lines, or from his own uncles, first cousins, or their descendants.

These clauses, embodied without essential modification in one renewal of the partnership deed after another, were to carry the patriarchal powers of Isaac Braithwaite far into the 20th century. They had the effect, probably at first unintentional, of confining the choice of partners within a very close circle indeed. Before long there were only certain branches of three families—Braithwaite, Barkworth, Savory—from whom full partners (as distinct from salaried partners) in Foster & Braithwaite could be drawn.

On the last day of 1876 Henry Waite died. He was in Egypt, and he had in his pocket, as his custom was when travelling, a Bank of England note for £1,000. It was stolen by a steward in the ship carrying his body to England, and later cashed on the Continent. Soon after Waite died, Charles Branch retired. With Waite's death and Branch's retirement, Isaac Braithwaite's new dispensation began to come into full effect and a change came over the character of the business which we discuss in Chapter VI.

REFERENCES

1 Biographical details from Joseph Foster of New Barnet—*A Pedigree of the Forsters and Fosters of the North of England and some of the Families connected with them*, 1871. I am indebted to Mr J. N. Savory for the reference.

2 J. Bevan Braithwaite, *Memoirs of Anna Braithwaite*, Headley Brothers, London, 1905, p. 152.

3 F&B Journal, 1825–1832. See also Harold Pollins, *Britain's*

Railways, David & Charles, 1971, p. 22; Jenks, *Migration of British Capital*, pp. 44–57; John Francis, *Stock Exchange*, pp. 267–278, 280–290.

4 F&B Private Ledgers to 1855.

5 Private Ledgers, Profit and Loss Account.

6 *Dod's Parliamentary Companion*, 1841.

7 R. K. Middlemas, *The Master Builders*, Hutchinson, 1963, p. 35.

8 Jenks, as (3), p. 144.

9 Middlemas, as (7), pp. 43, 73; Jenks, 164.

10 Pollins, as (3), pp. 35–40.

11 D. Morier Evans, *The Commercial Crisis 1847–1848*, London, 1849 (David & Charles Reprints), p. 3.

12 As (11), pp. 5, 13, and in general pp. 3–18; C. Duguid, *History of the Stock Exchange*, pp. 112–113; *Companion to the Almanac 1846*, Knight, London, pp. 72, 86, but see Pollins, as (3), p. 40, for slightly different figures.

13 *Companion*, as (12), pp. 70, 258; Evans, as (11), pp. 20–21.

14 *Companion to the Almanac 1847*, pp. 58, 95; *Companion*, 1848, p. 43—again the figures differ from those given by Pollins, though not seriously.

15 Mitchell & Dean, *British Historical Statistics*, p. 225.

16 Morgan & Thomas, *Stock Exchange*, Statistical Appendix, Table V, pp. 282–283.

17 *Companion* 1847, as (12), p. 259.

18 Private Ledgers.

19 Obituary, *Westmorland Gazette*, 1ii, 1890.

20 Private Ledgers, Profit and Loss Account.

21 MS reminiscences of J. N. F. Kellas, 7, in the firm's scrap book; Minutes of the Committee for General Purposes, Stock Exchange, 2 15 22v54 (Minutes nos 50, 62, 65).

22 Minutes as (21), 27iii38, 26iii52, 28iii53. Dates of Foster's retirement and death from MS note on a print of 1867 Partnership Deed.

23 Kellas, as (21), p. 6.

24 MS reminiscences of Cecil Braithwaite, in the firm's scrap book.

25 *Concise Dictionary of American History*, OUP, 1963, art. Railroads.

26 Dorothy Adler, *British Investment in American Railways 1834–*

1898, U.P. of Virginia, 1970, generally. Suceeding paragraphs rely heavily on Mrs Adler's book.

27 As (26), pp. 9–15; Duguid, as (12), p. 184.

28 Prospectus of the issue in *Economist*, 26vi52, p. 724.

29 Gustavus Myers, *History of the Great American Fortunes*, first published 1907, gives a lurid and detailed, if not totally objective, account of the railroad robber barons. References are to the First Modern Library edition, Random House, New York, 1936.

30 RC on the Stock Exchange, 1877, Minutes of Evidence, QQ 8306–8307.

31 P. W. Gates, *The Illinois Central Railroad and its Colonization Work*, OUP 1934, p. 73; Adler, as (26), pp. 20, 54–55, 90n.

32 Duguid, as (12), pp. 185–186.

33 D. Morier Evans, *The History of the Commercial Crisis 1857–1858 and the Stock Exchange Panic of 1859*, London, 1859 (David & Charles Reprints), p. 101.

34 F&B File 'American Lists'.

35 Evans, as (33), pp. 149–151; 163–164, quoting press reports.

36 Private Ledgers.

37 Adler, as (26), p. 71.

38 Duguid, as (12), pp. 151–152.

39 Private Ledgers.

40 *The Times* 9vi1866.

41 Myers, as (29), p. 417.

42 Duguid, as (12), p. 185.

43 As (30), QQ 3572–3573.

44 See, eg., Report of Foreign Loans Committee 1875; House of Commons Debate 20iii1877; Report of the Royal Commission on the Stock Exchange 1877 and Minutes of Evidence.

45 As (43); SE Minutes, as (21), 27iii54, 27iii55; Stock Exchange MS Membership Book.

46 Adler, as (26), 162.

47 As (30), QQ 8381–8383.

48 Robarts Lubbock, bankers, quoted in R. S. Sayers, *Lloyds Bank in the History of English Banking*, OUP (Clarendon), 1957, p. 134.

49 As (30), QQ 475–476.

50 As (30), Q 3461.

51 As (47).
52 Adler, as (26), p. 91.
53 Adler, as (26), p. 74; Sir John Clapham, *Economic History of Modern Britain* II, CUP 1932, 358.
54 F&B's General Account ledgers.
55 Private Ledgers.
56 As (30), QQ 8389-8391.
57 DNB.
58 Mrs Beeton's *Household Management*, 1895 Edn, p. 7.

Chapter V
Prosperity and Public Opinion: the Stock Exchange in late Victorian England

The Stock Exchange in the second half of the 19th century was an ebullient institution. There were 864 members in 1850: 1,979 in 1875, an increase of 129 per cent. By 1898/9 there were 4, 227, an increase since 1875 of 113 per cent. The building, enlarged and adapted, was never large enough, and the nominal value of securities quoted rose from £1,215.1 million in 1853 to £8,833.8 million fifty years later. As a business in its own right, the Stock Exchange was a profitable enterprise. In its first seventy-five years—from 1802 to 1877—the dividend on the shares, held in 1877 by about 500 'proprietors', averaged 20–21 per cent.[1]

In 1877 the Government Broker, J. H. Daniell, distinguished nine or ten 'markets', for different classes of securities, on the floor of 'the House.'[2] Twenty years earlier he would not have seen so many: twenty years later, more, and different, for the total business in quoted securities was not only growing in value but changing in composition, demonstrating as it did so political, social and economic change in Great Britain and in the world at large.

First, in the oldest and most dignified market—British Funds—the long late Victorian peace, its interruption in South Africa, and then preparations for the war to come were all reflected in the nominal value of securities quoted. The British Government, in those days, was only expected to borrow on a large scale in time of war or threat of war, and if peace endured it was not altogether fantastic to look forward to paying off the National Debt. The Debt rose to pay for the Crimean War (1854–1856), so between 1853 and 1863 the nominal value of British Funds quoted on the Stock Exchange rose from £853.6 million to £901.9 million. Then for thirty years the nominal value fell, going as low as £810.2 million in 1893. The Boer War increased the Debt, and so did the 'naval race' with Germany afterwards, and the figure rose to just over £1,013 million at the end of 1913.

Even at its 1913 figure, the total nominal value of British Funds quoted on the Stock Exchange was only fractionally higher than fifty years earlier: a commentary both on the security of Britain's position in the world—perhaps more apparent than real—and on the prevailing conception of the functions of government, which were not yet generally expected to include massive intervention in economic affairs or any very deep—and therefore expensive—concern for social welfare. Although by 1913 the theory was looking a little out of date, it was still widely held that the Government should confine itself to little more than foreign policy, including the defence of the realm, and the maintenance of law and order at home, so that private citizens could go tranquilly about their business. And that is the political reason behind the economic fact that between 1853 and 1913, while the total nominal value of quoted securities was expanding enormously, the value of British Funds fell from 70 per cent to 9 per cent of the whole.[3]

While 'the Funds' declined, the market in railway securities of all kinds, at home and abroad, grew rapidly, from about 18 per cent of the total value of securities quoted in 1853 to 37 per cent of the much larger total in 1913, and from about 1880 onward, or perhaps a little earlier, it was the largest group of securities, by value, on the Stock Exchange. Until the '80s 'Home Rails' were much more important than the securities of railways overseas. There were a great many companies—Foster & Braithwaite, between 1857 and 1895, dealt in the securities of sixty or so—and they were held in varying esteem. The Brecon & Merthyr Tydfil, for instance, or the Kendal & Windermere, were not classed with the London & North Western, and indeed J. H. Daniell, in 1877, placed only five lines—the London & North Western, the Lancashire & Yorkshire, the Midland, the London & South Western and the Great Western—in the 'heavy railway market' and the rest in other and, presumably, less distinguished categories.[4] The prior charges of the sounder companies were by this time well established as virtually risk-free, if unexciting, investments, and there was a wide field to choose from. The estate of a wealthy London soapmaker, for instance, in the '70s, had holdings in Great Eastern Preference shares.[5]

As the years went on, the spread of railways across the world was marked by the rise of Indian, Dominion and Colonial, American, and Foreign railway securities, offering every variety of opportunity for investment and speculation from the sober guaranteed stocks of the larger Indian lines to paper representing wild adventures in the United States, Central and South America. From the '90s onward the American section of the railway market was bigger than 'Home Rails'—and, indeed, bigger than British Funds—although by then the busiest phases of construction were past.

Apart from the railways, private enterprise in general was still not very plentifully represented by Stock Exchange securities until after the turn of the century, and even by 1913 public companies of all kinds provided barely more than 18 per cent of the total nominal value of quoted securities, whereas 'American Rails' alone provided over 15 per cent. The 1913 figure itself was much higher than the comparable figure twenty years earlier, because there was a considerable rise in company formation during the '90s. Before that, the move from private partnerships to limited companies, especially public companies, in British industry and commerce apart from railways, was still slow, so that between the '50s and the '80s the nominal value of company securities on the Stock Exchange only rose from 5 to 8 per cent of the total. From the '80s onward, Foster & Braithwaite were increasingly engaged in company promotion, but at that time and for many years afterwards it was an activity generally regarded, for good and sufficient reason, with grave suspicion.

Much larger than the market in company securities was the market, or rather the group of markets, in securities of Governments and public authorities other than the British Government. At home there was a small group of local authority stocks. In the British Empire there were securities issued by municipalities and by Dominion and colonial Governments. All these together—local authority stocks, Dominion and colonial stocks, municipal stocks in the Empire and outside—made up, by 1913, about 8 per cent of the total nominal value of quoted securities.

Alongside these were Foreign Loans. This market, which we have already briefly glanced at, had a history, running back into the 18th century, which had been full of disaster for many investors and full of profit for a few promoters. From the '50s, when they represented about 6 per cent of the total nominal value of quoted securities, Foreign Loans grew to a peak in the late '80s or early '90s, when they represented more than one-third of the total— 36 per cent in 1893, against 12 per cent for British Funds. By 1913 the nominal value of Foreign Loans was even greater, but the proportion of the total had fallen to about 28 per cent.

Many of these loans, based on the sound credit of the States that issued them, were good investments. Others were not. They were promoted, as the promoters very well knew, on behalf of bankrupt states to finance unlikely projects, and the methods used to launch them, which the Committee of the Stock Exchange connived at, were dishonest. Moreover the same methods were used by the less reputable promoters of companies. Thus it came about that although the Stock Exchange was flourishing in the late 19th century, it still had a very dubious reputation: so much so that in 1875 a Select Committee of the House of Commons investigated a particularly scandalous group of Latin American loans and in 1877 the Stock Exchange itself was enquired into by a Royal Commission.

In the launching of foreign loans—and in company promotion—the part played by the Stock Exchange was limited but essential. The mechanics of the operation were that the promoters of a loan, or a company, would take the loan, or the shares, at an agreed price and then make their profit from sales to the public. To do that they needed the kind of organised market which the Stock Exchange existed to provide.

The moral responsibility of the Stock Exchange arose from the power of the Committee, at their sole discretion, to grant or withold 'a settlement': that is, to fix a date on which bargains in newly launched stock or shares would be settled at officially quoted prices: the 'official quotation'. If no settlement was granted, these bargains would be void, there would be no market, and the launch would fail. The Committee maintained that the grant of a settlement implied no guarantee of the soundness of the securities concerned. It simply created a market within which investors might exercise their own judgement at their own risk. This was a view strictly in accordance with contemporary theories of individual responsibility and 'laissez-faire', but it was not widely accepted outside the Stock Exchange and the City. On the contrary, among the investing public there seems to have been a touching faith in the Stock Exchange Committee which, as the Report of the Committee on Foreign Loans put it, 'gives, by granting a quotation, a certain prestige to a loan'.[6]

The loans which attracted the attention of the House of Commons were raised between 1867 and 1872 on behalf of four ramshackle republics: Honduras, Santo Domingo, Costa Rica, Paraguay. The Select Committee's Report and the Minutes of Evidence on which it is based provide a searching and well-documented account of the world of Victorian high finance. In some corners of that world, and those by no means the most obscure, there was, in Anthony Trollope's phrase, 'dishonesty magnificent in its proportions',[7] and it is easy to see why the Stock Exchange was regarded with suspicion. Trollope had probably read the report of the Select Commitee, and a brief sketch of what they had to say about the Honduras loans will show that his remark was well founded.

The project for which Honduras sought to borrow money, on the face of it reputable enough and likely to attract investors, was to link the Atlantic to the Pacific by building a railway, 226 miles long, across the territory of the republic. What was not revealed was the opinion of two British Army officers who, in 1857–1858, had surveyed the route. Col. Stanton RE, the senior of the two, thought the railway 'could be made at a price, but ... he did not think it would pay.' G. C. Taylor, his junior, was far more outspoken: 'I had the greatest possible contempt for the country and for the loan.... I thought the thing was a swindle ... that the railway was a humbug; and that the whole thing was a humbug.'[8]

The project was unsound, and so was the country's credit. Honduras' foreign debt amounted to £120,000, a small enough sum, but most of it had been outstanding since 1825 and there was not the slightest prospect of any of it ever being paid. Honduras suffered from nearly every evil that can afflict a State: poverty, corruption; financial, political and administrative instability, dishonesty and confusion. There could be no possible basis for offering anything like a sound investment proposition.

When Honduras first came to the European market for money, in 1867, all these facts were either public knowledge or easily discoverable, and it is hardly surprising that the business was not handled by Barings or by Rothschilds. That did not matter very much. A great many firms in the 1860s were willing to try their skill at launching foreign loans: not only bankers but merchants and civil engineering contractors, and since their object was not long-term investment but a quick profit on the disposal of the stock they were not over-fastidious about the credit of borrowing States.

The representatives of the Government of Honduras made terms with Bischoffsheim & Goldschmidt. They had offices in London, Paris, Brussels and Frankfurt. Their London representative was Henry Louis Bischoffsheim and they had family connections with the *Société Générale*, the *Comptoir d'Escompte* and the *Banque de Paris et des Pays-Bas*.[9] They were thus linked, at a high level, with the speculative financial *expertise* of Second-Empire Paris, hardly a city of immaculate virtue. The brokers to the loan, in London, were P. Cazenove & Sons.

The first loan which this team, and their associates, set about raising was for £1 million, issued at 80, with a 10 per cent coupon, repayable at par over seventeen years, giving an annual yield of $12\frac{1}{2}$ per cent at a time when the yield on Consols, with no promise of repayment, was a little over 3 per cent.[10] The prospectus, issued early in November 1867, quoted an American admiral in praise of the 'salubrity, fertility, great variety of climate and productions, and valuable mineral resources' of the regions through which the railway was to run, but it said nothing of the financial state of Honduras. That was something which the Committee of the Stock Exchange might have been expected to query, because they had many years' experience of bankrupt states and had sometimes barred their securities from the market. When the prospectus was submitted, however, in support of a request for a settlement, they let it pass.

The Committee also let pass a certificate from Bischoffsheim & Goldschmidt, put in by Cazenoves, showing that

£501,100 of the loan, £74,782 3s 1d paid, had been allotted and that the remainder had been 'appropriated to the Continent'. On the strength of that, together with the prospectus and papers showing the powers of those who were authorised to contract the loan, the Committee granted a settlement.[11] Over the next few months, after the certificate had served its purpose in persuading the Committee to grant a settlement, £951,660 of the loan (including, presumably, the Continent's share) came back into the hands of the representatives of Honduras, leaving only £48,340 genuinely with the public.[12] Clearly, about 90 per cent of the 'allotments' certified to the Committee were the result of bogus sales, later cancelled. If these facts were not discoverable at the time, they were made abundantly clear in 1875, when the Select Committee investigated. Yet no dire consequences seem to have followed, either for Bischoffsheim & Goldschmidt or for Cazenoves.

In 1869, long before the 1867 loan was disposed of, the representatives of Honduras launched another loan, in Paris, for the equivalent in francs of the astonishing sum of £2,490,108 (nominal). The business of that loan was transferred to London after the Franco-Prussian War broke out, in the summer of 1870, and by that time there was yet a third loan under way, in London, for £2.5 million (nominal). By the summer of 1870, therefore, a state which three years earlier had been unable to pay debts of £120,000 was preparing to saddle itself with new debts of about £6 million, all at a high rate of interest and on onerous terms of repayment.

Nor was this all. In 1872 there was an attempt to launch yet another loan, this time for a railway which would carry ships across Honduras from one ocean to the other. The plan was devised by James Brunlees (1816–1892), later Sir James, and Edward Woods (1814–1903), each of whom served in the '80s as President of the Institution of Civil Engineers. They proposed that ships up to 200 feet long and weighing, laden, as much as 2,000 tons should be lifted hydraulically on to carriages with 240 wheels mounted on sixty bogies, running on three parallel tracks and hauled by a number of locomotives varying between six and ten, depending on the dampness of the rails. The scheme would have needed some £12 million, to be raised by a loan of £15 million at 80. A prospectus was issued on 22 May 1872.[13]

The proposal was killed by attacks from the Council of Foreign Bondholders and in the *Economist*, but it was hardly dead before plans were afoot to raise another loan in Paris. The launching of this one, after a Paris banking house had withdrawn, was entrusted to Captain Bedford Pim RN (retd), acting as Special Commissioner for the Republic of Honduras. The representatives of Honduras in Paris objected to this incursion, but the matter could have been arranged, according to Pim's later account, with a little judicious bribery. 'That is the sort of thing,' said the Captain stoutly, 'that English sailors are not much accustomed to, and I am afraid I used very strong language about it.' The result was 46 hours in a French jail for Captain Pim and no French loan for Honduras.[14] Pim's character emerged stainless, and by the time the Select Committee sat he was MP (Cons.) for Gravesend.

These proceedings were cynical and irresponsible to the last degree. There was never any possibility of any of the loans being properly serviced, and such payments as were made—they were only kept up long enough to serve the promoters' purposes—all came from subscribers' money. This irresponsibility was connived at by the Committee for General Purposes of the Stock Exchange. The prospectus of the 1870 London loan, issued on 20th June, said nothing of the 1867 loan; of the 1869 Paris loan; of the State debts outstanding ahead of these loans; or of the prior charges—which were heavy—on the securities offered for the new loan, which were all the revenues of 'the State and nation', the railway with 'all its chattels and returns', and all the territories and forests of the State, the fruits and products of which were to be remitted to Bischoffsheim & Goldschmidt for sale.[15] This remarkable exercise in *suppressio veri* seems to have survived the Committee's scrutiny, when settlement and quotation were applied for, without so much as the flutter of an eyelid.

The grant of a settlement was preceded and followed by the operation known as 'making a market': from the promoters' point of view, the most important activity of all, since their profits depended on it. Before the settlement it was necessary to create enough interest, or appearance of interest, in the stock to convince the Stock Exchange Committee that a respectable proportion had been allotted. Afterwards, and this was the really crucial period, the price of the stock had to be kept up until it was all profitably off the promoters' hands, including any they had been obliged to buy back.

In making a market for the various Honduras loans the central figure was C. J. Lefèvre, a 'financial agent' of Lombard Street with strong suspicion of a French criminal record in his background. From 'very embarrassed circumstances' between 1864 and 1868 he rose to showy affluence—'works of art by the greatest masters ... racehorses ...'—in 1870.[16] His method, broadly speaking (the agreements to which he was a party were very complicated), was to contract with the promoters of the loan to take stock at a low price and sell it at a high one. He would take it, for instance, at £68 12s (£68·60) for a £100 bond and sell at the issue price of £80 or higher, being only accountable to Honduras for £68 12s. During his work on the 1867 Loan, which lasted from July 1868 to June 1870, the quoted price never fell below 80 and it was frequently much higher—94 in November 1868, 88 in June 1870. His method was to get in touch with jobbers and brokers on the Stock Exchange, of which he was not a member, and manipulate a delicately balanced mechanism of sales and purchases. What part Cazenove played in all this is not clear. Several brokers' names were mentioned to the Select Committee, but not theirs.[17]

Once the stock was off the promoters' hands, their interest in it ceased. So did payments to investors, whether of capital or interest. They had all, in any case, been paid from bondholders' money. Genuine service of the loans would have required, by the time they were all out, £695,700 a year: a ludicrous liability for Honduras.[18] The price, of course, collapsed. The last payments for interest on the 1867 and 1870 loans were made on 1st July 1872, when prices were already sagging. It was no longer worth the promoters' while, nor Lefèvre's, to support the market, and by 1875 the stock was quoted at 6. Lefèvre decamped to France, from where he showed no eagerness at all to return and face the Select Committee.

H. L. Bischoffsheim was in London when the enquiry was going on, but a doctor certified that he was far too poorly to attend. The Honduras Minister, Don Carlos Gutierrez, was conveniently fenced about with diplomatic privilege.[19]

The interests of all those on the inside of these loans—Bischoffsheim & Goldschmidt, Cazenoves, Lefèvre, the Ministers of Honduras in Paris and London and, no doubt, various individuals in Honduras itself—were very carefully looked after. Elaborate agreements settled Lefèvre's terms and made commission and other payments to insiders the first charges on sums received. At least £200,000, nominal, was paid out in bonds to contractors, who no doubt sold while the selling was good.

All this was done at the expense of those who should have been the main beneficiaries of the loans: long-term investors and the State of Honduras. Speculators did well, but investors lost their money. In Honduras 53 miles of railway were built, trains began to run, and a good deal of preliminary work was done for further stretches of track, but on 15 May 1872 the contractors, evidently tired of applying for payments which never came, stopped work, The trains stopped, too, and the forest rushed back into the clearings. By 1875 all that Honduras had to show for the three loans was 53 miles of abandoned railway track, a pier at the Atlantic end of the line, and some earthworks and temporary buildings which the forest was rapidly swallowing. All that the bondholders had to show were some pieces of paper, doubtless decorative. The promoters of the loans, however, had done very well indeed.

The list of firms and individuals connected, in one way or another, with these Latin American loans shows how widespread their ramifications were in business circles and in public life. Bischoffsheim & Goldschmidt and Cazenoves, as well as others, were active in promoting the Santo Domingo loan of 1869. Don Carlos Gutierrez, as well as representing Honduras, acted as Minister and Special Commissioner for Costa Rica. Mullens & Marshall and Hichens Harrison, as well as Cazenoves, were brokers to various of the loans. The banking houses included J. S. Morgan and Emile Erlanger & Co. Peter Lawson & Son of London & Edinburgh, a firm of guano and seed merchants 'of the highest respectability' also tried their hand, not with notable success, at the foreign loan business, and so did the contractors Waring, McCandlish, who were more efficient.[20]

In launching two of these loans, to Paraguay in 1871 and 1872, two sharply contrasted individuals co-operated: Baron Grant (1830–1899) and Samuel Laing (1812–1897). Their careers provide an instructive commentary on Victorian attitudes to commercial morality.

Grant, by the standards of 'good society' in his day, was an outsider. He was born (in Dublin) Albert Gottheimer; his father was partner in 'a foreign "fancy" business' in London; he was educated partly in Paris; his title was Italian. He was probably the earliest large-scale company promoter, basing his activities on lists of clergy, widows and 'other small yet sanguine investors'. He made a great deal of money, flaunted his wealth, and lost it, going bankrupt in 1879. During his prosperity he sat in Parliament for Kidderminster and he performed 'a real service to the London public' by creating Leicester Square out of 'the neglected area of Leicester Fields, occupied by dead cats and other refuse'. This much merit Thomas Seccombe, the Balliol don from whose notice in the DNB these extracts are quoted, allows him, but he makes few other allowances: the tone of the notice is scathing throughout. No doubt Grant deserved it, but Seccombe's handling of Samuel Laing is very different.

Laing, though Scottish, was saved from being an outsider by academic success at Cambridge, where in 1831 he was second Wrangler and second Smith's prizeman, and by following a career which in many ways was a pattern of Victorian orthodoxy. He became a Fellow of St John's, went to the Bar, and then joined the civil service as secretary to the railway department of the Board of Trade from 1842 to 1846. From 1848 to 1855 he was very successful as Chairman and Managing Director of the London Brighton & South Coast Railway, having shrewdly and accurately estimated the passenger traffic possibilities of Brighton and other growing South Coast towns, and he held the same two posts again from 1867 to 1894. The stock of the railway was a speculator's favourite—Kellas mentions it in his reminiscences of Foster & Braithwaite—because so many stockbrokers lived along the line.

Laing sat as a Liberal in Parliament for Wick during the '50s and in 1859–1860 held office as Financial Secretary to the Treasury. That, again, was an orthodox appointment for a rising man, and in 1860 Palmerston sent him to India to 'doctor a sick budget with a deficit of six millions'. He came home again, highly successful, in 1865 and went back into Parliament, for Orkney and Shetland, in 1873. He held the seat until 1885: then retired and became an author of works on the controversy between science and religion and on other subjects, winning Seccombe's somewhat muted approval for being a good populariser.

Laing was thus a figure of the highest respectability: Grant was not. Nevertheless they collaborated in launching the Paraguay loans and were both richly rewarded at the bondholders' expense. This collaboration, followed by the disclosure of the Select Committee showing dishonesty in prospectuses and other documents, as well as thoroughly unprincipled operations on the Stock Exchange, seems to have harmed Laing's reputation not one whit: Seccombe does not mention the episode of the South American loans at all. Of course Laing, unlike Grant, was shrewd enough to avoid bankruptcy.

The report of the Select Committee, published in the summer of 1875, led on to a demand for a general investigation of the Stock Exchange. On 20 March 1877 the House of Commons passed a resolution calling for a Royal Commission. Disraeli's Conservative Government did not like the resolution very much but they were not prepared to stand in its way. The Chancellor of the Exchequer, Sir Stafford Northcote, said gloomily that 'he was not prepared to vote against the motion. At the same time, he did not believe any good would come of it.'[21]

The proposer and seconder of the motion were J. R. Yorke (1836–1912) and Sir Charles Russell VC (1826–1883), a Crimean veteran.[22] They were both Conservative country gentlemen, belonging to a class of MPs, now long extinct, who, holding Tory principles, might be considered the natural enemies of the Stock Exchange, the City of London, and high finance. Neither ever held office and it is a fair guess that each would have been insulted if anyone had called him a professional politician.

Professional politicians, however, is what two of their principal supporters were, and they sat on the other side of the House. One was Sir Henry James (1828–1911), Liberal MP for Taunton, who later became Lord James of Hereford. He had been Solicitor-General and Attorney-General under Gladstone. The other was Robert Lowe (1811–1892), later Viscount Sherbrooke, Liberal MP for

79

London University, who had been Gladstone's Chancellor of the Exchequer from 1868 to 1873.[23] It is easy to see why the Government would have much preferred Yorke and Russell to keep quiet.

Yorke said he thought the system under which the Stock Exchange was managed was not conducive to the public interest. 'A kind of "original sin",' he said, 'attached more or less to all those who took part in its proceedings'—a sweeping assertion, it might be thought—and 'until some radical reform occurred there was not a hope of better things.'

Russell joined in, saying that contractors for foreign loans 'were a body, not numerous, who, in the good old days, would have been called swindlers'. Echoing the views which Trollope expressed in *The Way We Live Now*, he said that a few years earlier 'they would not have been allowed to put their foot within the pale of respectable society, but nowadays respectable society not only tolerated, but toadied them. . . . It was the Stock Exchange, however, which, in his opinion, was chiefly responsible for the mischievous power which those contractors were able to exercise.'

Opposition to the motion came from quarters every bit as predictable as those which had produced it: from members representing the City and the interests of finance and banking. Both MPs for the City of London—Sir William Cotton (1822–1902), lately Lord Mayor, and J. G. Hubbard (1805–1889), a Director of the Bank of England—spoke against it. G. J. Goschen, the banker of German extraction who was later to be Lord Salisbury's Chancellor of the Exchequer, 'could hardly refrain from saying a word ... because his views were not on what might be called the popular side'. Neither of the two Members directly implicated in the foreign loans scandal, Captain Pim and Samuel Laing, said a word.

The view of the City interest, as put by Cotton and others, was that 'every man who purchased stock or shares did it, or ought to do it, after having well weighed the whole of the facts beforehand', and it was entirely his own fault if he lost money. The Stock Exchange certainly could not be blamed, and in any case it 'was open to the censorship of the Press ... and ... to the Law Courts'. It was not responsible for the rascally acts of defaulting foreign governments. Nor, said Cotton, was 'the constitution of the Stock Exchange ... responsible for the introduction of any company whatever'—company promotion was as great a source of anxiety as the promotion of foreign loans—and no company would be allowed a quotation until two-thirds of its shares had been subscribed for.

The manly assertion of liberal principles of individual responsibility sounded very well, and no doubt everything that Cotton and his friends said about the Stock Exchange was true, but it was disingenuous. They made no attempt to deal with the scandals of 'making a market', either in defence or disavowal, and they said nothing, either, of the remarkably lax way in which the Committee of the Stock Exchange had granted settlements for worthless foreign loans. They deplored the suggestion to appoint a Royal Commission as a blow to confidence, but the very substantial reasons for lack of confidence they left unexplored.[24]

A Royal Commission nevertheless sat and in 1878 issued a report, which, with massive Minutes of Evidence, provides the most detailed account of the composition and working of the Stock Exchange ever published. Moreover it remained a broadly reliable account for many years. Duguid, writing in 1904, said it still formed an 'admirable essay'[25] and in broad outline and in spirit, though not in detail, it probably held its accuracy much longer than that.

The Stock Exchange of the late 19th century emerges from the Royal Commission's pages as a flourishing, rapidly growing institution, its members prosperous and therefore rising in the social scale, but still with an equivocal reputation. When Isaac Braithwaite came to London in 1830 it would have been inconceivable for a connection of the Royal Family to become a member, yet forty-five years later Lord Walter Campbell, brother-in-law to Princess Louise, came in.[26] There was still an impression, nevertheless, that the stockbroker was on the shadowy border of respectable society. Escott, as we saw in Chapter I, compared him unfavourably with the merchant. In 1877 one of the members of the Royal Commission, discussing entrance qualifications, spoke of 'the very easy admission of a great many young men from the West end of the town ... who go and play at lawn tennis, and tell their friends "I can put you on to a good thing"', and went on to suggest that if that easy admission could be prevented 'you ... would do away with a great deal of the immorality into which this Commission is appointed to inquire'.[27] The Prince of Wales once visited 'the House', but probably a good many of his contemporaries would have considered his visit the reverse of a guarantee of respectability.

The wider and higher social acceptability of members of the Stock Exchange was important to them in business. The picture of affluent young men offering tips on tennis courts was probably drawn from life. Leaving the question of 'immorality' aside, it is clear that a great deal of Stock Exchange business was done informally and in the course of hospitality. Members of the Stock Exchange arranged their way of life accordingly, and a partner absent from the office was not necessarily neglecting the business of the firm. He might be attending to it effectively and lucratively round a dinner table or at a shoot.

One route to social success in England lay through sport, both in its older sense of hunting, shooting, fishing and racing and in its newer sense of the team games which were rising to a high pitch of popularity and organisation during the 1860s and '70s. Along with the rest of the well-to-do, newly risen, late Victorian middle class, members of the Stock Exchange, many of them with a public-school background, took to 'games' enthusiastically. By the end of the century the Stock Exchange could show a long list of names, most of which would mean very little to-day, of celebrated cricketers, footballers, tennis-players, runners, walkers and oarsmen.[28] Their enthusiasm no doubt was genuine but they cannot have been unaware that their abilities were business assets.

As a private club with restricted entrance, the Stock Exchange showed most of the attributes of that form of organisation. Apart from the written rules and unwritten code of conduct governing its business it had customs and traditions of its own—again one is reminded of the public schools—and its own notions of acceptable behaviour, thoroughly masculine in tone and characterised by a good deal of boisterousness and practical joking, particularly round about the fifth of November. Although capable of pompous ponderosity, particularly when frightened by its critics, the Victorian Stock Exchange was not in general an over-solemn institution, being well aware of its own frailties and well able to laugh at them.[29]

The politics of 'the House', overwhelmingly Conservative, might at moments of crisis be noisily expressed. There were demonstrations in support of the Government's anti-Russian policy when war seemed likely early in 1878; against Home Rule for Ireland; and to mark the outbreak of the Boer War on 11 October 1899. 'At the very minute when the Boer ultimatum expired ... the Royal Standard and the Union Jack were unfurled from the bench in the Rhodesian market, drawing all the members present to the spot. The singing of the National Anthem suggested itself. ... The second verse, dealing with Her Enemies, was sung even more enthusiastically than the first; and "Rule Britannia" followed. Great Britain was at war ... over a matter which closely affected the Stock Exchange.'[30]

Members of the Stock Exchange set a high value on the independence of their institution and its freedom from outside interference. Having been set up originally, as we have seen (pp. 3, 6 above), to conduct extra-legal activities, the Stock Exchange had developed its own discipline, and members had no intention of allowing the authority of the Committee of General Purposes to be over-ridden. In expressing this view they could look for support from orthodox economic opinion: that the State had a duty not to interfere in the running of private business. Nevertheless in their concentration on their own interests, to the exclusion of any wider interest, members of the Stock Exchange had something in common with members of trade unions, and the point was taken by a Liberal MP. 'What,' asked Sir Edward Watkin, 'is the Stock Exchange but a great Trades Union; and, as the House has inquired into the operation of many other Trades Unions, why should it not inquire into this one?'[31]

When the Royal Commission came to report, their sentiments turned out to be much the same as those of the Select Committee on Foreign Loans. They concentrated on company promotion, and especially on the dealings before allotment which were an essential part of the process of 'making a market' or of spoiling one. In the one case those interested in promoting a company would arrange for brokers to bid the price of shares up to a premium by heavy and mostly fictitious buying. In the other case opponents of the company would bear down the price of the shares by fictitious selling, running the risk of finding themselves at last without the shares they had undertaken to deliver and therefore obliged to cover their obligations at an uncomfortably high price.[32]

As in the case of foreign loans, dealings before allotment, whether intended to carry prices up or bear them down, were all aimed at the grant of a settlement by the Stock Exchange Committee. The Committee therefore bore a heavy responsibility, because if they granted a settlement for an unsound company there would be a crash afterwards, but if they refused to grant a settlement all bargains, including those entered into in good faith, would be void and the innocent would suffer with the guilty.[33]

Turning to a theme of complaint against the Stock Exchange which had been heard since its earliest days, the Royal Commission condemned speculation. 'We are satisfied', says their report, 'that gambling to an enormous extent does exist at the present day ... and that it is carried on both on the Stock Exchange and by persons outside of it who are not members.... The proceedings of the Bankruptcy Court are constantly bringing to light excesses of this kind, committed by persons who, having lost their money in trade, seek to re-establish themselves by desperate ventures in speculation.'[34]

Speculation Stock Exchange witnesses were prepared to defend. J. H. Daniell, the Government Broker, being fed with leading questions, agreed that by far the greater proportion of sales made by dealers were probably of stocks they did not hold. He went on to say that in his opinion the system was 'decidedly' beneficial to investors, because if the market were 'confined to merely buying in cases where a buyer wished to buy, and a seller wished to dispose of existing stock', the result would be 'that many people would not hold the securities which they do, there would be no market for them'. He enlarged the point by saying that if there were no speculative account in consols, bankers, insurance companies and others would not hold them, because they could not be sure of realizing their value when it suited them to do so. Speculation, that is to say, provided the level of activity needed to support investment or, as Daniell put it: '... the speculative market is the real foundation for the *bona fide* market'.[35]

Both bodies which investigated Stock Exchange practice in the 1870s found themselves, when they reported, in the same dilemma. They found plenty of evidence that members of the Stock Exchange connived at deplorable swindles in the issue of foreign loans and in company promotion. They found, also, that the Stock Exchange, a self-governing body, was unlikely to reform itself, but as good Victorian liberals they were unwilling to interfere with the Stock Exchange's management of its own affairs. That meant that any legislation that might be passed would be ineffective, because if any member failed to fulfil a bargain simply because it was illegal, the Stock Exchange would bring its own morality into play and expel him.

The dilemma was set out by the Select Committee on Foreign Loans in terms with which the Royal Commission, three years later, showed no disposition to disagree:

The Stock Exchange is a voluntary society.... It exists for the purpose of buying and selling, to which all its other functions are subordinate. There is no reason to doubt that as between its own members it administers substantial justice.... Such a body can hardly be interfered with by Parliament without losing that freedom of self-government which is the very life and soul of the institution.

The Committee which govern[s] the Stock Exchange ... is not fit for the exercise of judicial powers. Nor have your Committee [ie: the Select Committee] observed, in the evidence of members of the Stock Exchange ..., any very keen appreciation of the evils of the present manner of manipulating loans, or any fertility of resource in devising remedies ...

It was suggested by some witnesses that the evils ... would be met by legislation rendering illegal all contracts before allotment. But your Committee were distinctly told by the Chairman of the Stock Exchange Committee, that if such a law were framed that committee would expel a member who, having dealt in a loan before allotment, refused to fulfil his contract on the ground of its illegality. In all cases when a contract is made illegal for some reason which does not carry a moral taint, a legal debt is changed into a debt of honour, and thus the payment, instead of being prevented, is made more certain. So long as the Stock Exchange has the power of expelling one of its members without appeal or redress, it can be bound by no law which it does not choose to obey.[36]

The Select Committee had no intention of curtailing the Stock Exchange's power of expulsion. In words imbued with the essential spirit of *laissez-faire* liberalism, they then went on to say:

The business of the Stock Exchange is to buy and sell, not good securities only, but all securities that are dealt in, and it is hardly fair and hardly wise to entrust to it the power of supressing those questionable proposals by which it alone, of all the public, is certain to benefit.[37]

Since the Royal Commission as well as the Select Committee was broadly of this way of thinking, none but relatively minor reforms were suggested by either body, and nothing of any consequence was put into effect. Writing in 1900, with considerable complacency, Duguid observed '... although a quarter of a century has elapsed and the Stock Exchange still flourishes ... the main part of the [Royal Commission's] report has not been carried out'. Dealing before allotment, he said, was 'as rampant as ever' and the Committee still imparted prestige to a security by granting it quotation.[38] The Stock Exchange was still a place where members acted towards each other with the nicest sense of honour—and still a market which the public entered at their peril.

REFERENCES

1 Number of members from London Stock Exchange Commission—Report of the Commissioners—C2157/1878, HC Papers XIX 1878 (hereafter *RC Report*), p. 5, see also Duguid, *History of the Stock Exchange* (hereafter Duguid, *History*), p. 294; value of securities, Morgan & Thomas, *Stock Exchange*, Table V, p. 282; Stock Exchange profits, *RC Report* 6.
2 London Stock Exchange Commission—Minutes of Evidence—C 2157/1878—HC Papers XIX 1878 (hereafter *MoE*), QQ 494–501.
3 Morgan & Thomas, Table V.
4 *MoE* QQ 495–498.
5 John Knight Papers, Unilever House.

6 Report from the Select Committee on Loans to Foreign States, 1875 (hereafter *SC Report*), xlvi.
7 Anthony Trollope, *An Autobiography*, Collins (Fontana) 1962 (1st Edn, 1883), p. 274.
8 *SC Report* QQ 212–232; 2134–2136.
9 Jenks, *Migration of British Capital*, pp. 176, 317.
10 For prospectus see *SC Report*, Appendix, pp. 6–7; Morgan & Thomas, p. 278.
11 *SC Report*, p. vi; QQ 146–160; Appendix, 8.
12 As (11), pp. vi–vii.
13 As (11), pp. xxi–xxiii; Appendix, p. 120; Q 633.
14 As (11), Q 1900.
15 As (11), Appendix, p. 16 (prospectus).
16 As (11), QQ 2507–2513; 2575; pp. xiv–xv; QQ 2573–2574.
17 As (11), QQ 2228; 2765; 2588–2591; p. viii.
18 As (11), p. xxiv.
19 As (11), pp. xxv–xxvi.
20 As (11), generally.
21 Hansard, House of Commons Debates, 20 March 1877, p. 204.
22 *Who was Who* I; *DNB*.
23 *Who was Who* I; *DNB*.
24 See Hansard, as (21), pp. 203–238.
25 C. Duguid, *The Stock Exchange*, Methuen, 1904, p. 125.
26 Duguid, *History*, p. 172.
27 As (4), Q 293.
28 *The House on Sport*, 1898; as (26), p. 272.
29 See, amongst many similar publications, G. Duckworth-Atkin, *House Scraps*, privately printed, 1887.
30 As (26), p. 290.
31 As (21), p. 221.
32 *RC Report*, pp. 15–16.
33 As (32), pp. 18–19.
34 As (32), p. 20.
35 As (4), QQ 686; 842.
36 As (11), pp. xlvii–xlviii.
37 As (11), p. xlviii.
38 As (26), p. 209.

Chapter VI
Company Promotion

In 1880 Alfred Braithwaite, aged thirty-seven, died. Isaac, his father, was presented with the problem of replacing him: a problem as unexpected, no doubt, as it was unwelcome, for Isaac must have thought that by bringing Alfred and his brother Reginald into the firm he had provided amply for the succession. Of Isaac's three other sons one, Walter, was already dead and the other two were not available. Basil was established as a banker with Brown Janson. John Masterman Braithwaite (1846–1889) was a clergyman. Isaac, therefore, found himself obliged to call upon his considerable reserve force of nephews.

There were two already in the office. The elder, who came into the firm in 1876, was Joseph Bevan Braithwaite Jr (1855–1934), generally known to his partners as Joseph. He was one of the three sons (there were also six daughters) of Joseph Bevan Braithwaite Sr (1818–1905), a younger brother of Isaac, a barrister of some distinction, and a prominent Quaker. Joseph's mother, Martha (1823–1895), was the daughter of Joseph Ashby Gillett (1795–1853), a Quaker banker of Banbury, Oxon.[1]

Joseph Braithwaite went to school at Kendal, where the family still had strong roots, and then to the Quaker school at Grove House, Tottenham. He began to read for the Bar, but evidently the City had a stronger attraction and at the age of nineteen he switched to his uncle's firm. Like others in his family, he had a strong technical bent, and it carried him, as we shall see, towards the nascent electricity supply industry. It was to him that Isaac turned when Alfred died, and in 1880, at the age of twenty-five, he joined the partnership.

Cecil Braithwaite (1862–1948), who came into the office in 1879, was the son of George Foster Braithwaite of Kendal and of Mary Savory, daughter of a London goldsmith. Here again the Quaker tradition was strong, though it may have been diluted for Cecil by his education, not at a Quaker school but at Malvern College, one of the new and very self-conscious Victorian public schools. Isaac told Cecil not to expect a partnership because Alfred, Reginald and A. L. Noel were all ahead of him. The situation was completely altered, five years after Alfred's unexpected death, when Reginald also died at about the same age— thirty-eight. Cecil, aged twenty-four, took his place in 1886. In June 1888 Isaac Braithwaite, then aged seventy-seven, gave formal notice of retirement at the end of the year.[2] That had been foreseen, but not the blow, almost as heavy as the deaths of Alfred and of Reginald, which fell upon the partnership soon afterwards. This was the discovery that A. L. Noel stood in debt to the firm for a net amount of about £17,000, including drawings during 1888 of £6,750. His partners sent him a solicitor's letter demanding an explanation and Isaac forbade him either to come to the office or to make any further drawings. By October he had signed a deed providing for his retirement and for the reorganisation of the partnership. Remarks by Joseph at his retirement dinner in 1923, though guarded, make it tolerably clear that Noel's misdeeds put a severe strain on the resources of the firm.[3]

Noel had been a partner for twenty-eight years. Whether his conduct in 1888 was a sudden aberration or whether something of the sort had been going on for years, undetected, we shall never know. Nor shall we ever know precisely what brought him into debt, since the surviving letters and legal documents do not reveal it and the firm's various memoirists are discreet. All we can say is that Isaac seems to have felt some sort of responsibility and a lingering affection. In the Deed of Retirement he undertook to provide an annuity of £1,500 for two years and then £1,000 for three, to be paid to trustees for the benefit of Noel or, in certain circumstances including his bankruptcy, to his dependants. In his will Isaac left Noel 100 gns (£105.00), although to his other surviving ex-partner, Charles Branch, he left only 25.[4]

Isaac duly retired at the end of 1888. He had kept in daily touch with the office, but for years he had not been in the habit of visiting it, so that for the other partners his withdrawal probably had much less practical effect than the exit of Noel. For him they urgently needed a replacement, and in August 1888, at the height of the crisis, an offer was made to the banker Basil Braithwaite. With some reluctance, he turned it down, thinking it best, as he put it, '*not to make a change from a position where I have been so many years*'.[5] The offer did not come from Basil's father, Isaac, but from his uncle, J. B. Braithwaite Sr: a curiously indirect approach.

No son of Isaac being available, the partners turned, as their articles required, to other relations. Ronald Herbert Savory (1856–1931), who had joined Foster & Braithwaite in 1883 after four years' experience with another firm of brokers, became a partner. He was Isaac's nephew by his sister Mary Caroline (1818–1887) and fifth son of Joseph Savory (1808–1879), who had followed his father and uncle into the family's goldsmith's business and was extremely well-to-do. His mother was the twin sister of J. B. Braithwaite Sr, and his father's sister Mary (1823–1909) was Cecil Braithwaite's mother, so that when Savory joined the partnership the family connexions within it became very intricate. His partnership he owed, to some extent, to the influence of his elder brother Joseph (1843–1921), a City magnate of whom we shall have much more to say. He was sent, like his brothers, to Harrow, from

91

which he emerged with the social and sporting tastes of the upper middle class of his day. He was fond of country life; of cricket; of shooting, tastes that could be readily put to use in getting business for the firm.[6]

In the course of ten years the premature deaths of Alfred and of Reginald and the unorthodox behaviour of A. L. Noel transformed the Foster & Braithwaite partnership and ruined, probably, Isaac's plans for the succession. He had no doubt expected to leave his two sons at the head of the business when he retired. Instead, there was a triumvirate of much younger cousins—Joseph Braithwaite, Cecil Braithwaite, and R. H. Savory—all of them, in 1890, comfortably under forty and one, Cecil, only twenty-eight. Moreover Joseph Braithwaite, by the same concatenation of death and dereliction of duty, became senior partner when Isaac went: a position which in the early '80s he surely cannot have expected to reach for many years, if ever.

This third generation of Foster & Braithwaite's management, following on from Isaac and from the founder, James Foster, were very different in tone from their predecessors. They represented the social level which members of the Stock Exchange were reaching in the latter part of the 19th century, and in moving away from the Northern Quakerism of their forebears towards the way of life of the well-to-do circles of the Establishment they followed a path much frequented by the rising middle class of late Victorian England. In business, they turned the attention of the firm more strongly than ever before towards the field of company promotion and company finance.

In looking at this aspect of Foster & Braithwaite's business, it is essential to be clear about the nature of the firm's function in 'bringing out' a company and to distinguish it from the function of individual partners, especially Joseph. Foster & Braithwaite were not merchant bankers, finding funds from their own resources (except in a minor way) or by borrowing them. Nor were they concerned to set a business up, physically, or to run it as a going concern. They were part of the machinery required by the Stock Exchange for discharging its central function of providing a market for securities, and what they did for a new issue was to find buyers for some portion of the securities offered.

Joseph Braithwaite as an individual developed for himself a role in the electricity supply industry which went far beyond his position as a stockbroker. He was a close associate of Emil Garcke (1856–1930), a German electrical engineer who became a British subject in 1880 and was prominent in the British electrical industry from 1888 onward.[7] He was elected a Member of the Institution of Electrical Engineers in 1893 which, although qualifying examinations were not then set, suggests a more than amateur degree of technical competence. At one time or another he was Chairman of most of the electrical companies which his firm 'brought out', and his interest in their affairs, not being confined to putting their securities on the market, was lasting, not intermittent. He came to be regarded far more as a leading figure in the electricity supply industry than as a stockbroker, and the *Financial Times* remarked in an obituary that he 'seldom entered the Stock Exchange'.[8] Nevertheless there was a close link between his position as an individual and the activities of the firm in bringing new issues to market, which depended very heavily on the confidence felt in Joseph Braithwaite and his partners by those concerned with the floating of companies.

There were two principal ways in which a broker could bring securities to market, and examples of each are to be found in Foster & Braithwaite's records. The firm might circulate prospectuses to clients, asking for applications to be returned so that the firm might, as the standard letter accompanying prospectuses put it, 'have pleasure in endeavouring to secure an allotment'.[9] The firm would previously have been promised the right to make allotments

93

from a given portion of the issue, and if the issue went well they would scale down applications at their discretion, generally granting small applications in full and larger ones as they thought good. Payment would be by commission on the allotments made.

The other method was underwriting: that is, the firm would subscribe for some portion of an issue of securities, undertaking either to find buyers for the whole or, in default, to take up any unsold remainder. It was apparently an innovation in the'80s, for the financier H. Osborne O'Hagan, a contemporary of Joseph Braithwaite, claimed to have originated it.[10] The firm's reward was by way of commission on sales and an underwriting fee calculated as a percentage of the nominal value of the securities, as, for instance, when in 1889 Foster & Braithwaite took up £25,000 1st Mortgage 6 per cent Gold Bonds of the Kansas Waterworks for 1 per cent commission plus 5 per cent for underwriting.[11] Other underwriting fees during the same year varied between $4\frac{1}{4}$ and 5 per cent.

Foster & Braithwaite seem to have gone into company promotion for the first time at the start of a boom in electric lighting which enlivened the Stock Exchange in the early 1880s. By this time there was no doubt that electric lighting would have a promising future in the long run, but in the short run it was an exceedingly risky industry for an investor to enter. He had to make up his mind, in the first place, whether the future lay with arc lighting, and if so, which of several rival systems to back, or whether the new incandescent 'bulbs', being developed independently and competitively by Joseph Swan and Thomas Edison, were shortly going to sweep arc lights into obsolescence. Secondly, neither the legal system nor the system of local government in the United Kingdom had been developed with the laying of electric cables in mind, and the outlook for distribution was obscure.

When, therefore, at the end of 1880 Foster & Braithwaite acted as brokers to the issue of £400,000 capital by the Anglo-American Brush Electric Light Corporation, they were entering a highly speculative field. As *The Times* remarked, 'this appears a very large sum to embark in such an enterprise at the present stage of development which electric lighting has reached'.[12] The Corporation was formed to acquire, for the United Kingdom and a large number of other countries, patent rights originating with Charles F. Brush, an American, also to take over contracts for supplying 'dynamo machines, lamps, and carbons, forming the complete system of lighting known as the Brush system'. The Corporation's profits were expected to come from four main sources: sales of the Brush system; sales of patent rights; 'the letting-out of lights worked from central stations'; contracts with corporations and other public bodies and with firms and individuals. The Brush system was already in use, or contracted for, in two new men-of-war (*Minotaur* and *Inflexible*), at Woolwich Arsenal, in museums at South Kensington and Jermyn Street, and in various railway establishments, including Paddington Station, and factories.[13]

How Foster & Braithwaite were attracted, in the first place, to electric lighting we cannot now tell. The junior partner, Joseph Braithwaite, who later became Chairman of the Brush company (after it was re-named Brush Electrical Engineering Co.) may have played some part, but he was not on the original Board. The Chairman was Captain Sir Henry Tyler MP (1827–1908), a retired officer of the Royal Engineers who, like other Victorian sapper officers, had put to very good civilian use his early technological education at the Royal Military Academy. The other Directors included two more army officers and the Corporation's resident technical expert, Thomas J. Montgomery, an American.

The firm, according to Cecil Braithwaite's memoirs, took up on its own account 1,000 fully-paid £10 Brush shares. That may have been the result of optimistic underwriting but Cecil gives the impression that it arose from faith in the company's future. If so, that faith was severely tested in 1882, for the shares had to stand the racket of a very volatile market indeed, enthusiastically stirred up by amateur and professional speculators. Helped by the well-publicised activities of an electrical engineer called Hammond, whose own company was installing Brush apparatus in London and elsewhere, Brush shares rose very sharply—Cecil says, to £60 for fully-paid £10 shares—largely because investors expected the company to make handsome profits from concessions granted to companies formed to work Brush patents in various parts of the country.[14]

O'Hagan, one of the professionals, gives an account in his autobiography of the Metropolitan Brush Company which he promoted, in association with Morton Rose, bankers, to take a Brush licence for 'the whole of the metropolitan area'. The shares did very well for a time and O'Hagan, by selling out near the top, made £100,000, leaving others, as he says, to ' "hold the baby" '. By that time 'bears' were already campaigning against Brush, Hammond, and Metropolitan Brush, and panic set in.

Cecil Braithwaite's account of the same boom and slump, though different from O'Hagan's, is not necessarily incompatible with it. He says that Brush promoted 'a whole family of subsidiaries' which collapsed because 'the Law at that time made it next to impossible to work'. He was probably referring to the Electric Lighting Act, 1882, which frightened investors and entrepreneurs by giving local authorities an option to buy electricity undertakings after only 21 years (extended to 42 years in 1888). Whatever the state of the law, there is no doubt that many unsound schemes were launched and the market in general became over-excited, as it has done many times before and since.

Anglo-American Brush was not intrinsically unsound, as it demonstrated by its survival, but its shares collapsed along with the rest and Foster & Braithwaite were among those whom O'Hagan left 'holding the baby'. The firm's income, which had risen in 1880 to £82,482, a higher figure than ever before, dropped away by 1884 to £20,511, which was no doubt what prompted Isaac to write mournfully to Joseph, in 1885, 'I have no doubt that what you say about having to practise economy is true. It has grieved me much that the business has not been what I expected, during the last 2 years: but I think the worst is over, and that we shall see better times. I have great confidence in the result of cheerful patient care and diligence.' It is to be hoped that Joseph had, too, because his income from the partnership dropped from £3,000 in 1881 to £600 in 1884. Already, however, stockbroking was not his only source of livelihood. 'I consider', his uncle wrote, 'any fees you may receive for your directorships are strictly your own. I never thought otherwise.'[15]

Isaac expressed his own view of company promotion in an undated sheet of notes in his own hand, headed 'Requisites for bringing out new Companies.' He laid down that the object should be 'a legitimate one for a public Company—i.e. in its nature and magnitude'; that the Directors should be 'men of position': that there should be 'a well grounded expectation of its proving remunerative'; that the requirements of the Stock Exchange should be complied with. He added that 'foreign companies newly set on foot' should have 'an English board of respectable position', and that before Foster & Braithwaite undertook foreign enterprises, 'particularly mines', they should send out their own inspector.[16] These are unexceptionable sentiments, especially the last, but why Isaac should have felt moved to put them on paper we do not know. Probably he was anxious for his firm not to give grounds for any of the suspicion with which the whole business of company promotion was widely regarded.

For some years after the collapse of the electric lighting boom Foster & Braithwaite seem to have kept clear of company promotion and the like. As soon as Isaac retired, however, there was an outbreak of activity, strongly suggesting that Joseph and Cecil had been waiting for their uncle to go. In the first six months of 1889 Foster & Braithwaite were concerned in one way or another with placing or underwriting securities of City of London & Southwark Subway Co. (later City & South London Railway, the world's first electric tube railway)[17]; Kansas Waterworks; City of Santa Fé, Argentina; Caranero Railway & Navigation Co., Venezuela; a shipping company promoted by Money, Wigram; Anglo-American Brush; City of Cordoba, Argentina; Northern Pacific Railroad; and Stroud Water Company.[18]

This may have been a wholly exceptional burst of activity—our evidence for it is an isolated packet of papers, evidently preserved for some special purpose—but it shows which way the thoughts of Isaac's younger partners were turning. Very soon they were 'bringing out' issues of securities not as occasional ventures but as part of the regular business of the firm.

In this kind of work the partners no doubt had their principles, as Isaac had before them, but they had no illusions. 'In these days', writes Cecil with engaging frankness, presumably referring to the 1890s and early 1900s, 'it was quite customary for say half a dozen men to get together and form a Company. No prospectus was produced till many days after dealings had commenced, and the procedure was as follows. The Broker appointed by the promoting group went into the market and told his friends that he was bringing out a Company to exploit, we will say, a Gold Mine. He—the Broker—explained what the Company was, and let his friends have some shares, with probably a call of more. He then arranged to have the shares bid for in order to attract attention, his friends in the market having "Bated [sic] the Swim" among their friends. At this stage the Company was not even registered. If the operation was successful, and a good market was established, a prospectus was then advertised, and nominally the public had a chance of subscribing. I say nominally, because if the shares already stood at a good premium, the public had very little chance of obtaining any. A special settlement was then applied for, which unless there was opposition generally went through. If the efforts of the group in the market failed to make the shares go, and be popular, often nothing more was heard of it.'

'I could give an account,' says Cecil darkly, 'of the now historical Corner in the shares of Warners Safe Cure, whose shares went to £60 each and ruined many members of the House.' This was a particular example of the kind of market-rigging he describes in general terms. Warner's Safe Cure was a liquid sold at 2s 9d (in 1909) for about 8 fl. oz. It was advertised 'For Kidney and Liver and Bright's disease and jaundice, gravel, stone' and a long list of other complaints and was to be taken in doses of one tablespoonful five or six times a day. An analysis made for the British Medical Association showed that the main constituent—about 10 per cent—was pure alcohol, which no doubt helped it down, five or six times a day, but there was no reason to suppose that it would do any of the things that were claimed for it.[19] Nevertheless, when 35,000 Ordinary shares in the company which owned the Cure were issued in November 1889 they rose rapidly, reaching £50 premium—the figure quoted by Cecil—on 21 April 1890. Dealings then ceased, and the price collapsed. One member of the Stock Exchange, known as Wicked William (his name was William Morris) was said to have died of a broken heart. Charges of conspiracy failed, but nobody believed that they were groundless.[20]

This was a world which would have been familiar to the promoters of the scandalous South American loans of the early '70s, and at least one of them, Bischoffsheim & Goldschmidt, moved into it, being associated, Cecil says, with some of the electricity issues. Nor did matters improve as time went on. In some ways, they grew worse. The Companies Act 1900 tightened the rules about prospectuses, so more companies, according to Duguid, were floated without them. They did not then qualify for official quotation, but if you were only in them for quick profits on a rigged market that might not matter very much.[21]

Foster & Braithwaite's most consistent interest was in companies formed either for electrical engineering, or for the distribution of electric power in towns, or for electric traction. In the first category was the Brush Electrical Engineering Company; in the second, City of London Electric Lighting (1891), County of London and Brush Provincial Electric Lighting (1894), and companies formed in 1899 and 1905, in England, to operate electricity undertakings in Melbourne and Adelaide; in the third category was British Electric Traction, formed in 1896 with electric trams chiefly in mind.

The role of the financier in setting up these companies was emphasised early on, by the formation, in 1890, of The Electric and General Investment Corporation. There was again something of a boom in electric lighting, and the Corporation's prospectus asserted that 'the principal Electrical Manufacturing and Contracting Firms in this country, as well as abroad' were getting more business offered to them than they could handle, and that they had 'neither the time nor the facilities for ... promoting and financing new electrical undertakings'. This was what the Corporation was being set up to do. 'THE CORPORATION', says the Prospectus in capital letters, 'WILL NOT ITSELF MANUFACTURE ANY ELECTRICAL APPLIANCES; NEITHER WILL IT EMPLOY ANY STAFF FOR CARRYING OUT ANY INSTALLATION CONTRACTS, BUT IT WILL RESTRICT ITSELF TO THE FINANCIAL AND COMMERCIAL OPERATIONS OF ASSISTING IN THE PROMOTION AND DEVELOPMENT OF ELECTRICAL UNDERTAKINGS.' Profits were expected from underwriting commissions; from the acquisition and realisation of concessions, Provisional Orders* etc.; from interest and profits on investments; and from 'remuneration for services in examining, reporting on, and assisting the promotion and development of electrical undertakings'. The first issue of capital was £100,000 in 10,000 Ordinary shares of £10 each and £1,000 in 100 Founders' shares of £10 each, carrying a right to half the surplus profits each year after payment of 8 per cent on the Ordinary capital.[22]

This cluster of electrical companies had the makings of a self-sufficient group, with its own manufacturing, technical and financial services, and at a rather later period it might have been fused together under a holding company, instead of remaining a relatively loose-jointed mutual aid society. Even as it was, Electric & General provided some of the services of a holding company. It presided over the birth of at least three of the other companies—City of London, County of London, BET—providing some of the early finance and, at least in the case of the County company, obtaining the all-important Provisional Orders, without which there would have been no point in launching the company. It also undertook negotiations for power station sites and arrangements for the public issue of shares. These services might be rendered directly or, as in the cases of the City company and BET, through a 'Pioneer' company, launched with enough capital to take the essential preliminary steps, which would sell out to the much larger permanent company when the way had been sufficiently prepared.[23]

Intermediate services such as these, which of course had to be paid for, were among the features of company promotion which contemporary critics deplored, often with good reason, because they felt that investors' money was going anywhere but into the undertaking for which it was ostensibly provided.[24] Electric & General certainly did not

---

* Ie.: Provisional Orders by the Board of Trade, under the Electric Lighting Acts 1882 and 1888, granted to local authorities, companies or persons for supplying electricity in particular localities, and giving them the rights necessary to do so.

undervalue their services. They charged the County company £15,000, in cash or shares at the company's option, against an issue of £200,000 capital. BET, raising £300,000, agreed to pay Electric & General £10,000 in cash and to issue to shareholders in the Pioneer company, which E&G had set up, blocks of shares in BET equivalent to their Pioneer holdings. These payments were substantial in relation to the capital of the companies concerned, and there may have been other payments which the prospectuses do not reveal. On the other hand there was no element of fraud about them, as there was about too many of the practices of company promoters of the day. The services rendered were real, perhaps indispensable, and E&G played a genuine part in bringing the electricity supply industry into existence.

On the manufacturing side, E&G, all the supply companies and BET had a special relationship with Brush Electrical Engineering Company. They were careful not to give Brush a monopoly, but the contracts disclosed in the various prospectuses show that they intended to give Brush a preference. The City of London Electric Lighting Co. was formed specifically to enter into construction contracts with Brush—and with the Laing Wharton & Down Construction Syndicate—for lighting the City. The County company's prospectus disclosed a contract with Brush for equipment, as well as a tripartite contract for an unspecified purpose with E&G as well as with Brush, and the prospectus of the Electric Lighting & Traction Company of Australia showed an array of contracts between itself, various local authorities, E&G and Brush.

Finally, as well as the contractual and financial links between the electricity companies, the personal links were strong as well. There were twenty original Directors of the half-dozen companies set up between the formation of Electric & General in 1890 and of Adelaide Electric Supply in 1905. Of these twenty, four were on the Boards of two of the companies, two were on the boards of three, and one—Joseph Braithwaite—was on the Boards of four, being the original Chairman of three: County of London, Electric Lighting & Traction of Australia, and Adelaide Electric Supply. He was also Chairman of Brush Electrical Engineering before 1901, and of the City company and E&G from 1906 until he died.[25]

Of the remaining Directors of the six companies, it may not be uncharitable to assume that four noblemen among them, headed by the eighth Duke of Marlborough, first Chairman of E&G, were valued chiefly as purveyors of social tone. Among the rest Sir C. Rivers Wilson (1831–1916), first Chairman of BET, was a representative figure of the high Victorian Establishment—Eton and Balliol, the Treasury, the Suez Canal Company, the Grand Trunk Railway of Canada, briefly Finance Minister to the Khédive of Egypt. The first Chairman of the City company, Joseph Savory, besides being brother to R. H. Savory and cousin to Cecil Braithwaite, was Lord Mayor of London in 1890–1891. Emil Garcke and J. S. Sellon were both electrical engineers. Garcke was an original Director of two of the companies—E&G and BET—and Sellon of three—the County company and the two Australian companies—and no doubt it was in this way that technical policy was co-ordinated, just as the ubiquity of Joseph Braithwaite presumably helped with the co-ordination of finance.

Joseph Savory's connection with E&G and with the City of London Electric Lighting Company in the year when he was Lord Mayor had embarrassing consequences. As Lord Mayor he was *ex officio* Chairman of the Commissioners of Sewers who, by what looks like some very subtle bureaucratic train of thought—sewer gas, perhaps?—had become the lighting authority for the City. Savory seems genuinely to have forgotten his position with the Commissioners, but he can hardly have forgotten he was Lord Mayor, and his proceedings could be made to look like municipal jobbery at the highest level, particularly when it could be shown that he and his relations had done very well out of the financial manœuvres connected with the launch of the City of London company. The whole episode was made public in a periodical called *London*. Sir Joseph, as by then he was, took exception to the tone of the article and brought an action for libel. He won, and it was made clear that he had not been corrupt, only careless, but the jury made it clear that they had no sympathy with him by awarding derisory damages of one farthing. 'Of course', as the *Financial News* put it, 'no man who holds shares in a concern that promotes a company [Sir Joseph was a shareholder in E&G] can expect any consideration at the hands of a jury in the present state of the public mind.'[26]

The electrical companies have been discussed at length because in building them up Joseph Braithwaite, his partners, and the firm, exercising separate but closely interlinked and mutually supporting functions, were taking part in what is generally regarded as the Stock Exchange's most constructive role in the economy: raising capital for productive enterprise, in this case the manufacture of electrical equipment, the distribution of electricity, and the running of electric tramways. We have examined, as far as surviving records will allow, the machinery by which the capital was raised and reached the companies. It came largely by way of the activities of Foster & Braithwaite in and around the Stock Exchange and through Electric & General. The question remains: who put up the capital? Who were the capitalists, and how were they persuaded to put their money into these particular enterprises?

It is fairly clear that this most important part of the process depended very heavily on the personal connexions of Joseph Braithwaite and his partners. It was the confidence placed in them by rich men or rich banking houses which determined the matter. Among the banking houses Rothschilds was certainly one, until in 1895 or thereabouts, according to Dudley Smith's memoirs, Lord Rothschild sent a messenger to say that he wished to see Joseph, to which Joseph replied: 'Well—I am here': a reply which is said to have ended the Rothschild connection. There was a long-standing link with J. S. Morgan, which between 1900 and 1902 led Foster & Braithwaite on to the periphery of a battlefield where a struggle was being fought out between American interests for parliamentary powers to build tube railways in London.[27] It is highly probable, but by no means certain, that Morgan may have taken an interest in the electrical businesses. Cecil's memoirs mention the Continental house of Bischoffsheim & Goldschmidt, which we have met before, and also Sir Ernest Cassel (1852–1921), saying that both were introduced to Foster & Braithwaite by George Herring.

George Herring (1832–1906), whom Cecil Braithwaite refers to as 'a power of strength' behind Foster & Braithwaite, has found posthumous respectability in the Dictionary of National Biography as a 'philanthropist', and the Salvation Army, among other worthy institutions, had reason to be grateful to him. He was known as The Bloater, his origins were obscure, and it was said that after he had presided at a meeting the floor would be littered with the h's he had dropped. He established himself, first, as a bookmaker, 'associated', in the words of Bramwell Booth, 'with that class of doubtful characters who frequent race meetings', but with a personal reputation for impeccable honesty, at any rate towards his clients. His clients were of the highest class, socially, which no doubt smoothed his path into the City where, in association with H. L. Bischoffsheim, he went into foreign loans and the promotion of securities generally.[28]

Herring and Joseph Braithwaite, a curiously assorted pair, did much business together. Cecil mentions that Herring arranged an issue of £600,000 5 per cent debentures for the Bombay Electric Company, carrying a bonus of Ordinary shares, and that at Herring's invitation Joseph and Cecil joined him in a syndicate with Sir Ernest Cassel and Bischoffsheim, each party (Joseph and Cecil acting as one, presumably in the name of the firm) taking £150,000. Cecil says they made a very big profit. There is nothing to show how Herring came into the financing of the electrical industry or how large his interests were in the companies promoted by Foster & Braithwaite and their associates, but they were large enough to bring him the Chairmanship of Electric & General and of the City of London Electric Lighting Co., both of which he was holding when he died. He left £1.3 million.

The '90s were busy years for company promoters generally and for Foster & Braithwaite in particular. So far as it is possible to tell from surviving records, which may not be complete, there were only three years—1892, 1893, 1895—between 1889 and 1900, both inclusive, when the firm did not 'bring out' at least one company. Most of their promotions, as we have seen, were in electric supply or traction, but besides those the firm brought out British & Colonial Explosives Co. Ltd in 1889, Lever Brothers Limited in 1894, two companies operating in Australia in 1897 and 1898, and De Keyser's Royal Hotel Ltd in 1900. In the early years of the new century they were associated with the launch of Piccadilly Hotel Limited in 1904, Deccan Goldfields in 1905, and Harrisons & Crosfields in 1908.

British & Colonial Explosives and Deccan Goldfields look like highly speculative issues. The explosives company was one of a number formed to take advantage of the lapse, in 1881, of Alfred Nobel's dynamite patents.[29] One of its Directors, Col. J. L. du Plat Taylor (d 1904), was a Birmingham man well known in the explosives industry. The rest were Cornishmen and Foster & Braithwaite may have come into the project through their business with Cornish bankers. It was no doubt formed, as other similar companies were, to be an expensive nuisance to the Nobel-Dynamite Trust, but it made no permanent mark on the trade. The purpose of forming The Deccan Development Company, the prospectus says, was 'to open out selected old workings or other locations' on goldfields

near the Kistna River in the West of the Nizam of Hydera-
bad's dominions. During the '90s Indian goldmines had
been fashionable and some had made a lot of money.[30]
It seems unlikely that the Deccan Company ever did.
Lever Brothers was a very different proposition.
William Lever (1851–1925) burst into the soap trade in
1885, formed a private company in 1890, and by 1894
claimed to have the largest soapworks in the world. He
put 75,000 £10 5 per cent Cumulative Preference shares
on the market, keeping much the greater part of a like
amount of Ordinary capital in his own hands, where it
stayed until he died. The issue was a huge success: four
times over-subscribed. Foster & Braithwaite were sole
brokers in London, but R. J. Tilney & Co. acted in Liverpool and Lawson & Ormerod in Manchester. Between
1894 and 1914 Levers went time and again to the market
for Preference capital, always with success. Foster &
Braithwaite were brokers to the company for many years,
but Lever never took them so closely into his confidence
as Sir Robert Nivison (1849–1930: Lord Glendyne 1922),
who was his principal adviser in the City for over twenty
years.[31]

Harrisons & Crosfields, though less spectacular than
Levers, were equally sound. Their merchants' business,
chiefly in the Far East, dated from 1841 but the partners
did not form a limited company until 1908. When they
did, they did it in a manner thoroughly characteristic of
late Victorian company formation. They put 150,000 £1
5 per cent Cumulative Preferred Ordinary on the market
but they kept in their own hands 150,000 £1 Preferred
Ordinary shares and arranged an issue of 150,000 Management shares of 1s (5p) each to the Directors. They thus
gained access to wider sources of capital while keeping the
control of the business, undiluted, in their own hands.

The two Australian companies were both in business in
Sydney, Farmer & Co. as drapers, mercers and furniture
warehousemen, and W. & A. McArthur Ltd as ware-

housemen. Both had strong English connexion, Farmers through Sir William Farmer (1831–1908) who had been Sheriff of London when Joseph Savory was Lord Mayor, and McArthurs through W. A. McArthur, born in Australia in 1857, who was a Liberal MP. Once again, no Ordinary capital was put on the market and there is no doubt that the businesses remained under the control of the former owners. They are chiefly interesting to us because we know the terms on which Foster & Braithwaite agreed to act as brokers, having previously been closely consulted on the method of financing each company.

Farmers issued £133,340 in £10 6 per cent Cumulative Preference shares. Foster & Braithwaite agreed to circularise their clients and asked Sir William Farmer to place £80,000 at their disposal for allotment, leaving £53,340 'for distribution amongst any of your personal friends, or those specially interested in the business, and the general public.'[32] They do not appear to have asked for any consideration apart from the brokerage, being presumably confident of the success of the issue. It was, in fact, oversubscribed, and F&B's allotment list survives to show how the applications were scaled down. McArthur's issue was underwritten, half by Foster & Braithwaite and half by the Manchester firm, Lawson & Ormerod. The terms for each firm were the same. Each was to underwrite £37,500 4½ per cent Debenture Stock and 37,500 £10 5½ per cent Cumulative Preference shares, and each was to have 500 guineas (£525), £2,437 10s (£2,437·50) underwriting commission (2½ per cent on the Debentures; 4 per cent on the shares), and 10s (50p) per share on allotments made under the firm's stamp.[33] So far as we know, the issue was a success.

These were two sound, if small, issues. For the Deccan Goldfields issue the underwriting agreement also survives. It provides for Foster & Braithwaite to underwrite 66,667 £1 Ordinary shares out of £91,667 for a brokerage of 3d per share. They were also granted an option on the remain-

108

ing shares, at par, for three years. Foster & Braithwaite proceeded briskly to make agreements with sub-underwriters, which survive, but whether either they or their sub-underwriters saw fit to exercise their share options we cannot tell.[34]

Alongside the series of company promotions, the business of the firm went on roughly according to the pattern set in earlier years, particularly the highly successful decade of the '70s. That is to say, the two main sources of income were commission dealings and dealings on General Account.

The commission side of the business still relied heavily on business from the banks, and the firm's ledgers, in the early years of the 20th century, show clearly the trend towards amalgamation and the gobbling up of small and not so small banks, with their trains of branches, by bigger ones. Between 1900 and 1906 Foster & Braithwaite dealt with 36 country branches of Barclays Bank: between 1907 and 1911, with 71. The Devon & Cornwall Bank, with 57 of whose branches Foster & Braithwaite had dealings, was taken over by Lloyds Bank in 1906. Barclays, in the same part of the country, about the same date, took over Bolitho Williams Foster Coode Grylls & Co.—itself an amalgamation of considerable proportions—and, in the North, the York Union Bank with at least sixteen branches. The list could be considerably extended.

Apart from the banks, Foster & Braithwaite's clients were chiefly private individuals, as they had been during the 19th century and continued to be until the onslaught on private wealth after the 2nd World War. On the pages of the ledgers there is a sparse scattering of titles and a good many military and naval ranks. Clergymen are fairly numerous: so are women, married and unmarried. Occasionally well-known names occur—John Bright, W. E. Forster (the Quaker connection, no doubt, in both cases), Thomas Hardy, W. H. Lever, J. H., later Sir John, Clapham, the Cambridge historian—but in general the entries are not eloquent. They simply tell us what we should expect, that most of the clients came from the Forsyte level of society and upwards. Probably many—country parsons, for instance, and maiden ladies, were of no great wealth.

The investment lists which the firm sent to clients between 1903 and 1914 graded suggested securities according to yield and riskiness. In 1903 four groupings were suggested:

A. Trustee securities yielding $3-3\frac{1}{2}$ per cent, including the Guaranteed Stock of the large home railways.

B. First-class securities, not necessarily coming with the terms of the Act, yielding $3\frac{1}{2}-4\frac{1}{2}$ per cent, including junior stock of the large home railway companies; certain American railroads (Baltimore & Ohio, Pennsylvania); Rhodesia Railways; Great Western Ordinary.

C. Sound commercial preference and debenture stocks yielding $4\frac{1}{2}-5\frac{1}{2}$ per cent, including Lever Brothers 5 per cent Cumulative Preferred Ordinary; County of London and Brush Provincial Electric Lighting Debentures and Cumulative Preferred Ordinary; British Electric Traction 6 per cent Cumulative Preferred; J. & E. Hall 6 per cent Cumulative Preferred.

D. 'Securities yielding a high rate of interest and consequently of a more speculative character'—that is, yielding $5\frac{1}{2}$ per cent or more, and including the Ordinary shares of British Electric Traction, City of London Electric Lighting, and Baltimore & Ohio RR.

Recommendations over the years followed very much in the spirit underlying these classifications, although the classifications themselves altered from time to time. Ordinary shares, except in the soundest home railway companies, were regarded as speculative even in businesses of the highest class, and it is evident that the ordinary investor's portfolio, insofar as it contained industrials at all, was expected to carry chiefly fixed-interest securities. Imperial and foreign securities, including 'somewhat speculative' issues by Chinese, South American and Mexican railways, frequently appeared in the lists, following the fashion of the day, but in 1913, after 'political and financial events in Europe, China, Mexico and Brazil, and even in Canada', 'the absurdly exaggerated bias in favour of foreign investments was severely commented on'. Railway shares, at home, in the Empire, and elsewhere—especially in America—were the most numerous of the securities listed, followed probably by public utilities of various kinds. Joseph Braithwaite's electrical interests were brought to clients' notice, especially, in 1908, the shares of the supply companies in London 'now that . . . fears of outside competition have been effectually removed by the rejection by Parliament of all competitive Bills'. By April 1911 investors were familiar enough with oil shares for Foster & Braithwaite to comment on them as a class, remarking that 'the growing interest in the use of Oil as a fuel and the advance in price of Oil which has recently taken place will, we anticipate, lead to renewed activity before long'.

Throughout the series, the economic and political crises in international affairs are commented upon. So is the growing social and industrial unrest at home: as, for instance, when a circular issued on 28 December 1911 remarks: 'The HOME RAILWAY market closes the year once more under the shadow of labour unrest.' The last circular but one in the collection, issued on 1 October 1914, reports that the Stock Exchange is closed indefinitely and 'all dealings at present are being carried on for cash'.

As against commission business, the riskiness of dealings on General Account showed up sharply in the last thirty years before the Great War. In 1882, 1883 and 1884 there were successive yearly losses on General Account of £6,760, £29,273, and £2,818 against profits from commission business of £19,465, £12,727 and £13,036. Matters were put right by drawing heavily on the contingency fund, built up in the prosperous years 1879–1881, but it becomes evident why Joseph had to economise. He was not, however, thereby discouraged from General Account dealings: nor were his cousins. The '90s, on the whole, were good years for the Stock Exchange, running up to the boom in South African mining shares, known as the 'Kaffir Boom', which ran for two or three years from 1896 onward in the heady atmosphere of late Victorian imperialism, and the firm admitted new partners.

Alfred Montgomery Barkworth (1873–1943), Isaac's grandson through his daughter Louisa, was admitted in 1897. John Sidney Braithwaite (1874–1948), son of the Rev. J. M. Braithwaite, Isaac's third son, became a partner in 1899.

There were also partners who were not relations. One, William Huntingdon Beeman, had been admitted in 1880, presumably on Isaac's authority, as a full partner with a share in the capital. Once Isaac was gone, no such arrangement was possible. James Douglas Lewis, admitted in 1895 after twenty-five years as an authorised clerk, and Philip Isaac Beeman, a brother of W. H. Beeman, were both 'salaried partners' on quite different terms from the members of the family.

In these years the annual balance of the General Account fluctuated widely—between £3,662 in 1890 and £67,596 in 1897—but it always showed a profit. The profits from commission business fluctuated far less, never falling below £16,609 (1892) and never rising above £28,954 (1895), so they always at least provided a substantial safety net. In most years, they did more. In six of the ten years 1890 to 1900 the balance brought into the partners' ledger from the Commission Account was greater than the balance from General Account.

Both Kellas and Cecil Braithwaite mention that Foster & Braithwaite in these years were money lenders, willing to finance clients' speculations on a considerable scale. 'To show how large our money-lending business was,' Cecil remarks, 'the Firm used to consistently make the Office expenses out of it.' That would mean £13,000 to £20,000 a year, varying a good deal with circumstances: equivalent, say, to the balance of the Commission Account in a leanish year.

The firm's position in the '90s, then, was sound though scarcely dynamic. If there was growth, it is not reflected in surviving figures. The income recorded in the partners' ledgers, which may or may not include the proceeds of company promotion, ran up to £92,204 (gross) in 1897—much the highest figure in the 19th century—but taking one year with another it was scarcely as high as in the '70s.

Foster & Braithwaite 1898–1914

Credit and Debit Balances shown in Partners' Ledgers (Profit & Loss Account)

	General Account		Commission Account	Interest Account	
	Credit	Debit	Credit	Credit	Debit
1898	£33,045		£23,946		£1,966
1899	20,692		29,584		1,822
1900	19,634		23,796		7,610
1901	32,803		34,087		7,210
1902	37,163		26,253		7,226
1903		£7,830	24,685		8,891
1904	41,633		22,468		9,087
1905	37,781		24,095		7,525
1906		28,694	20,655		12,987
1907		8,866	17,849		16,574
1908	24,801		24,167	£4,870	
1909	21,924		33,984	3,460	
1910	38,455		42,526	7,915	
1911	16,164		24,236	8,678	
1912	30,779		30,470	7,349	
1913		12,635	21,470	9,158	
1914	— (a) —		20,405	5,895	

(a) From 1914 onward 'General Account' no longer appears as an item in the partners' profit & loss account except from 1920 to 1929.

113

The best years of the decade were at the end, and Joseph's dividends, from a level of £3,000 to £5,000 in the early '90s, ran upwards to a peak of £20,814 in 1897. Dividends for the other partners, of course, kept pace in proportion to their holdings in the firm. It was open to all the partners to add to their resources—or not, as the case might be— by private investment and speculation. R. H. Savory did well enough out of the Kaffir boom to set himself up very handsomely at Chertsey in Surrey, and a little later he bought the Kelling Hall estate, one of the best sporting properties in Norfolk.

A year or two before the turn of the century this comfortable situation began to alter for the worse. First, the interest account, from which the partners' interest on their capital and certain other commitments were met, ran into deficit in 1898 and obstinately stayed there. Such a thing had occasionally happened before, but never for more than a year or two. Now the figures remained red for ten years. The partners continued to receive interest, but where the money came from is not obvious.

Next, the General Account showed losses—the first since 1884—in 1903, again in 1906 and 1907, and again in 1913. In other years it showed profits, sometimes considerable, but in the fourteen years from 1901 to 1914 the credit balance on General Account was greater than the balance on Commission Account in only four years. In 1903, 1913 and 1914 no dividends were declared on partners' capital, and in 1906 and 1907 a levy was made to meet losses: in 1906 at the rate of £97 a share: in 1907 at £230. At that rate, in 1907, Joseph was debited with £6,670, Cecil with £6,440, R. H. Savory with £3,220, and the two junior partners—A. M. Barkworth and J. S. Braithwaite—with £2,760 each.

These figures (set out in full in the table) make two things clear. First, between 1898 and 1914 the firm ran into serious trouble. Secondly, the trouble arose entirely from the side of their activities represented by the General

Account and not at all from their business as brokers, for the Commission Account remained healthily in credit throughout. The extent of the firm's losses are made plain enough in the partners' ledgers, but not their precise causes. What emerges, however, from other surviving papers, is that the losses of 1906 and 1907 were so serious that the firm's own resources, even after the levies on the partners, were not great enough to put matters right. The firm had to borrow, and it speedily began to appear that its assets were not great enough to secure the loans that would be needed. At least £9,000 was raised from the Drapers' Company, secured on the lease of the firm's premises at 27 Austin Friars. After that, Sir Joseph Savory and Basil Braithwaite came to the rescue, not by lending money, but by depositing securities which the firm could pledge against loans from other sources.

The first hint we have of this arrangement—damaging, surely, to the partners' self esteem—is a letter written by Joseph Braithwaite to Sir Joseph on 21 December 1908, giving a list of securities held by the firm on Sir Joseph's account. Then on 23 September 1909 Joseph Braithwaite formally acknowledged the loan of securities to the market value of £15,000, secured like the Drapers' loan, but presumably ranking after it, on the lease of 27 Austin Friars.

This loan was originally for nine months, but until after the Great War it became a permanent feature of Foster & Braithwaite's finances. At the suggestion of R. H. Savory, securities valued at £16,000 were added to it in January 1914 and at some unspecified date earlier than September 1915 it was reinforced by a similar loan from Basil Braithwaite. For the use of Sir Joseph's securities Foster & Braithwaite made a token payment of £210 a year. Sir Joseph continued to receive the dividends, and he kept the right to sell securities provided he made equivalent replacements. Presumably the terms of Basil's loan were much the same.[35]

115

Meanwhile, in spite of good results between 1908 and 1912, including very good results indeed in 1910, the firm slid further towards disaster, largely as a result of two projects undertaken several years earlier. Both were adventures in company finance, more appropriate to the business of a merchant banker than of a stockbroker, and in each case the firm entered into capital commitments which, when things went wrong, overstrained its resources and endangered its credit.

There was first the affair of the Piccadilly Hotel. It had its origins in Sir Joseph Savory's acquaintance with Sir Polydore De Keyser (1832–1897), a naturalised British citizen, of Belgian descent, who was Lord Mayor of London in 1887–1888. He was a hotelier by trade, and in 1874 he opened De Keyser's Royal Hotel Blackfriars, a 400-room establishment intended to cater for the Continental traffic which then passed through Blackfriars Station on the London, Chatham and Dover Railway. After Sir Polydore's death, in 1901, De Keyser's Royal Hotel was launched to take over the business. Foster & Braithwaite were brokers to the issue and R. H. Savory joined the Board.

In 1904 a new hotel company was launched: the Piccadilly Hotel Limited. Savory was on the Board, his Norfolk neighbour G. M. Chamberlin was Chairman, and the General Manager (also on the Board) was P. W. De Keyser. The issued share capital was £650,035 and besides that the Company issued £500,000 Prior Lien Debenture Stock and £700,000 4½ per cent Mortgage Debenture Stock. The Prior Lien Debentures were all taken up by six insurance companies. One of them was the Norwich Union with which R. H. Savory had close personal connexions. Foster & Braithwaite took up, on General Account, £22,500 of the Mortgage Debenture Stock: a holding which they increased to £25,540 and then reduced to £24,242. They also invested £20,010 in 6,600 £5 5½ per cent Preference shares and 4,000 £1 Ordinary.[36]

The hotel, with an exterior by Norman Shaw, with a telephone, a radiator and an electric clock in every bedroom, with sixty suites decorated and furnished by Libertys, opened in May 1908 after a discreet visit by the Prince and Princess of Wales.[37] It then promptly ran short of cash and in August the debenture holders put in a Receiver and Manager.

Among the debenture holders Joseph Braithwaite was very prominent, representing not only Foster & Braithwaite but also the Gas, Water & General Investment Trust which he had taken a large part in founding. A committee was formed which worked hard to reorganise the hotel company's finances in a way which would save something for themselves, the shareholders and the creditors. The committee's efforts were cut short by an offer from H. Mallaby Deeley to buy the entire undertaking, in which about £1·6 million had been invested, for £500,000. The insurance companies, holding Prior Lien Debentures, seeing a chance of getting their investment back, refused to have any part in the scheme of reorganisation, which would have required them to leave their money in the company and to reinforce it with more. On 14 December 1909 the sale of the Piccadilly Hotel to Mallaby Deeley was completed. Foster & Braithwaite lost their entire investment, Debentures, Preference shares, Ordinary shares and all, and indirectly, no doubt, they suffered through the losses of Gas, Water & General.[38] It can hardly be a matter of pure chance that as Mallaby Deeley closed in they were arranging to borrow Sir Joseph Savory's securities.

As the Piccadilly Hotel venture ran its course an even worse disaster was building up, arising from the enthusiasm of Cecil and Sidney Braithwaite—particularly Sidney—for a scheme put forward, during a visit to London in the autumn of 1901, by an American railroad promoter, Arthur E. Stilwell (1859–1928).[39] He intended to link Kansas City with the Pacific Ocean at Topolobampo in

117

Mexico, 1,600 miles away on the shore of the Gulf of California, whence ships would set up a new trade route to the Far East. Topolobampo had no port, so Stilwell proposed to build one. He called his line the Kansas City, Mexico & Orient Railway.

By the time he conceived the KCM&O, Stilwell was an experienced railroad promoter, and he had to his credit one major achievement: the Kansas City Pittsburgh & Gulf Railroad, a line some 700 miles long connecting Kansas City with the Gulf of Mexico at Port Arthur, newly built and named after Arthur E. Stilwell, which came fully into operation in 1899. The history of the port and of the line was turbulent; the line's finances were disastrous, though not for Stilwell personally; and in 1900 the KCP&G was taken over by the Kansas City Southern Railway, organised for the purpose by Stilwell's rivals, who were determined to get him out. Nevertheless when Stilwell arrived in Europe in 1901, seeking capital, he was not without credibility as a railroad promoter, and amid the ferocious exuberance of American railroad finance his record could hardly be called calamitous. But American railroad finance was an extremely dangerous field to enter, as Foster & Braithwaite had two generations of experience to show.

Stilwell's business activities were laced with religious enthusiasm of a peculiarly American kind, founded on the Christian Science of Mary Baker Eddy. One of his methods of attracting investors was to take parties of them on tour in a luxurious private train, and among the luxuries was a harmonium. It came into action after Stilwell had addressed the assembled capitalists on the glowing prospects of the KCM&O, when he would hand out hymn books and lead the singing, accompanied by his secretary on the harmonium.[40]

Perhaps it was this aspect of Stilwell's character which attracted Sidney Braithwaite, for this son of a clergyman became such an enthusiast for Christian Science that he eventually devoted his life to it.[41] However that may be,

8 De Keyser's Royal Hotel, opened in 1874 near Blackfriars Railway Station. Foster & Braithwaite were associated with a later de Keyser enterprise, the Piccadilly Hotel, opened in 1908. See pp. 116–117. (*Illustration by courtesy of Unilever Ltd*)

9 Ronald Savory (1856–1931). Partner 1890–1919. See Chapters VI and VII.

10 Joseph Braithwaite (1855–1934). Partner 1880. Senior Partner 1888–1922. See Chapters VI and VII.

11 Cecil Braithwaite (1862–1948). Partner 1886. Senior Partner 1922–1938.
See Chapters VI, VII and VIII.

27. Austin Friars
1931

12 27 Austin Friars, as rebuilt in 1931, where Foster & Braithwaite had their offices from 1863 until 1970. See pp. 176–177.

13 Sir John Braithwaite (1884–1973). Partner 1908. Senior Partner 1963–1971. Chairman of the Council of the Stock Exchange 1949–1959. See Chapters VII, VIII and IX. (*Photograph: Douglas Glass*)

14 King George VI, Queen Elizabeth and Princess Margaret at the Stock
Exchange, 23 May 1951. On the War Memorial Gallery stand the Chairman
of the Stock Exchange Council, John Braithwaite (next the King) and the
two Deputy Chairmen, Frank Doran (next Queen Elizabeth) and Dick
Twining (next Princess Margaret). This was King George's last public
appearance.

15 The Family Partners 1975. *Left to right:* David Braithwaite, Michael Savory, Jeremy Braithwaite. (*Photograph: Baron*)

he and Cecil Braithwaite joined the London Finance Committee of the KCM&O in the autumn of 1901. In March 1902 several members of the Committee—it is not clear whether either of the Braithwaites was among them—went back with Stilwell to Kansas City and then toured the proposed route of the line in Mexico, singing hymns, presumably, as they went. Between 1902 and 1911 such tours were many times repeated, mostly for the benefit of English investors.[42]

On the first of these tours, says Keith L. Bryant, Stilwell's biographer, 'the Englishmen agreed to make large purchases of stock'.[43] Sidney became a Vice-President of KCM&O, representing the English interest generally. His colleagues on the Board included several eminent American railroad men, several bankers, the President of Western Union Telegraph, and W. C. Procter of Procter & Gamble, a large American soap firm. It would seem, therefore, that Sidney's enthusiasm for Arthur E. Stilwell was shared by investors who should have been well qualified to know what they were about. He may have been daring: he was scarcely eccentric.

Foster & Braithwaite quite early began to deal on behalf of clients in KCM&O securities, having no doubt brought them to their clients' notice in the first place, and probably Sidney and Cecil invested as individuals: perhaps other partners also. There is no sign of the firm's money going into KCM&O, however, until April 1907, when the railroad's securities appear for the first time in the General Account ledger.

The firm received a fee for underwriting 4 per cent 1st Mortgage 50-year Gold Bonds, due for redemption in 1951, and they appear to have bought bonds on their own behalf, for two calls are recorded for bonds to a nominal value of $64,000 (say £12,800).[44] The bonds were issued to provide security for 7-year bonds issued by an associated company, Mexico & Orient Townsite Company, to finance the development of towns along the route:[45] not, it might be thought, an enterprise for investors seeking a quiet mind and a good night's sleep, especially since a good many of the towns were in Mexico.

Mexico & Orient Townsite was just one of an intertwined group of companies, some for construction, some for equipment, some for property, of which KCM&O itself was the head and front. In this, as in many other ways, KCM&O was a typical American railroad. Its finances relied heavily on mortgaging the assets of the line and on property deals: so much on the latter, indeed, that the running of trains began to look like a means to an end rather than an end in itself. Also, and this again was nothing out of the ordinary, the expenses of construction were consistently under-estimated so that the line was at the same time short of capital and, being incomplete, in no position to generate enough revenue to service fresh capital or even capital which had already been raised.

It was this situation, tending always towards insolvency—a condition very familiar to American railroad men (Bryant says that 65 per cent of all American railroads went into receivership between 1893 and 1898)[46]—in which Foster & Braithwaite became enmeshed. Stilwell, working desperately to prop up his edifice, issued more and more securities and devised schemes to protect those already in issue. He had a good deal of success. Bryant says that English investors, assisted by 'a number of leading London brokerage firms', 'pumped money into the "Orient"': a phrase which appears to mean £308,642 in securities by 1911.[47]

Foster & Braithwaite showed their faith in the recommendations which they made to their clients by building up substantial holdings on General Account. By 1913 they had $155,957 50-year Gold Bonds plus $15,000 'certificates', though what they certified is not made plain. These bonds carried rights to bonus issues, and by 1912 the firm had acquired, partly or wholly by this means, 1,323.8 4 per cent Non-cumulative Preference shares plus 432 options, the sum invested in the whole being shown as £6,863 1s 9d. They held also, almost certainly as a result of bonus issues, 1,485 Common [Ordinary] shares, and they had a large holding, probably 33,500, of Secured 6 per cent Sterling Convertible 5 per cent notes. There is no evidence of any of these securities ever paying a dividend, except by way of more securites, except £946 7s 6d occasionally paid on the 6 per cent notes.[48]

They also joined a number of syndicates. The first was the '£60,000 Syndicate' of 1909, in which they bought one share for £5,500. This was a profitable investment, being paid off in 1910 for £6,000 plus interest (£220 16s 11d), 100 Preference shares valued at £540 and 100 Common shares valued at £360. The other three syndicates seem to have been more expensive and less fortunate. In the 'S1 million Syndicate', also of 1909, Foster & Braithwaite subscribed, apparently, S250,000—sub-divided, no doubt among their clients—and they appear to have received dividends in cash and bonds, but to exactly what amount it is impossible to say. To the 'London Syndicate' of 1910 they subscribed £5,980 ($36,000) without traceable return, and to the '$3 million Syndicate', 1910–1913, they subscribed without return no less than £14,565 3s 4d in ten instalments. Bryant says that this last syndicate was formed to complete a section of the KCM&O in Texas, between San Angelo and Alpine, 'and failed when subscribers refused to pay their assessments'.[49] Some subscribers evidently took a different view of their obligations from Foster & Braithwaite's.

The finances of the KCM&O were complicated but the reason for its distress was simple: too much loan capital, too little profit. By 1912 or thereabouts the company had $12·5 million preference stock in issue (against $12,264,135 Common) and $18·9 million first mortgage bonds, of which only $6 million had been sold for cash, the remainder being held by construction companies. There was also £200,000 in 6 per cent five-year notes, due for redemption in 1913 and the company owed $1,618,885 for equipment. To service all that, the KCM&O had produced a surplus only in three years: 1904, 1905, 1907.[50]

By 1910 bankruptcy could not be far away, and the revolution which broke out in Mexico in that year brought it speedily nearer. In March 1912 the KCM&O's American creditors, with the backing of the English bond-holders, had the line put into receivership.[51]

Stilwell, protesting volubly about the unfairness of it all, retreated gradually into an eccentric world of his own in which spiritualism held a large place and 'Brownies' appeared to him in dreams—as they had done, he revealed in 1921, at moments of decision during his active business life.[52] He died in 1928. The KCM&O was eventually completed, though not in his lifetime or in the form or under the name that he had devised. In 1961 the Mexican end of it, under Mexican ownership, was at last carried through the formidable barrier of the Sierra Madre to the sea at Topolobampo, giving the through connection that Stilwell had intended, but at a cost, for the mountain section alone, of $88 million. Stilwell's idea was not unsound, but the execution of it, as he should surely have understood, called for vastly greater resources than he could ever command.

REFERENCES

1 Audrey M. Taylor, *Gilletts*, OUP (Clarendon) 1964, pp. 221, 226–227.
2 Isaac Braithwaite to his Partners, 25vi88, F&B Private Papers.
3 Isaac Braithwaite to A. L. Noel, 3viii88; Ashurst Morris Crisp to A. L. Noel, 3viii88; A. L. Noel's Deed of Retirement, 18x88. All in F&B Private Papers. Partners' Minute Book, 11 January 1923.
4 *Westmorland Gazette*, undated cutting.
5 Basil Braithwaite to J. B. Braithwaite Sr, 13viii88. F&B Private Papers.

6 For information on R. H. Savory and his son R. C. Savory I am deeply indebted to Mr J. N. Savory, son and grandson. I have also used Professor D. L. Savory's 'Joseph Savory of Montpellier and his Descendants', reprinted from *Proc Huguenot Soc of London* XVII No 5 and XVIII No 1, 1946 and 1947, and Helen P. Savory's *Memoir of Joseph P. Savory*, n.d., privately printed, kindly lent to me by Mr C. Berry Savory.

7 *Who was Who III*: private information from Dr L. Hannah.

8 *Financial Times* 1xii34.

9 Foster & Braithwaite's Investment Lists.

10 H. Osborne O'Hagan, *Leaves from my Life*, 2 vols, John Lane, The Bodley Head, 1929, I, 149.

11 Letter to Slaughter & May, 20iii89, F&B Private Papers.

12 *The Times* 14xii80.

13 From the Prospectus published in *The Times*.

14 Memoirs of Cecil Braithwaite in F&B's Scrapbook; as (10), pp. 118–125.

15 Isaac Braithwaite to J. B. Braithwaite Jr 30iii85. F&B Private Papers.

16 'Requisites for bringing out new Companies', F&B Private Papers.

17 T. C. Barker and Michael Robbins, *A History of London Transport*, 2 vols, Allen & Unwin 1963, 1974, I, pp. 305–315.

18 All in F&B Private Papers.

19 *Secret Remedies*, BMA London, 1909, p. 72.

20 Duguid, *History of the Stock Exchange*, pp. 233–234.

21 Duguid, *Stock Exchange*, p. 112.

22 Third Proof of Prospectus, F&B Private Papers.

23 Prospectus—'City' company, 7ii91; 'County' company, 3iv94; BET., 11xi96.

24 See, eg., Report of Company Law Amendment Committee, C7779 of 1895, 85.

25 Obituary notice, *J. Inst. Elect. Eng.* 77, 1935, 888.

26 *Financial News*, undated cutting.

27 As (17), II, p. 77.

28 *Who was Who I; DNB;* Memoirs of C. Dudley Smith in F&B Scrapbook; Bramwell Booth, *Echoes and Memories*, Hodder & Stoughton 1925, 110–112.

29 W. J. Reader, *ICI*, I, pp. 72–73.

30 Nancy Crathorne, *Tennant's Stalk*, Macmillan, 1973, 139–140.
31 Lever Brothers Limited Prospectus; Wilson, *Unilever*, I, pp. 45, 252–259.
32 Foster & Braithwaite to Sir William Farmer, 1ii97, F&B Private Papers.
33 Underwriting agreement, F&B Private Papers.
34 Underwriting agreements, main and subsidiary, F&B Private Papers.
35 Correspondence with Sir Joseph Savory and Basil Braithwaite. F&B Private Papers.
36 Piccadilly Hotel papers in F&B Private Papers; GA Ledger T 1896.
37 *The Times*, 5v08.
38 Piccadilly Hotel Papers, esp. Minute Book of the Debenture Holders' Committee, 1908–1909. F&B Private Papers.
39 Keith L. Bryant Jr, *Arthur E. Stilwell*, Vanderbilt University Press, Nashville, 1971, provides an indispensable foundation for the succeeding narrative.
40 As (39), 184–185.
41 Memoirs of H. W. Hart, F&B Scrapbook.
42 As (39), pp. 183–184.
43 As (39), p. 183.
44 General Account Ledger U, 1906.
45 As (39), p. 192.
46 As (39), p. 154.
47 As (39), p. 210.
48 As (44).
49 As (39), p. 216.
50 As (49).
51 As (39), p. 217.
52 As (39), p. 238.

Chapter VII
The Anxious Years, 1908–1922

Between 1908 and 1914 a new generation of partners began to come into Foster & Braithwaite. Joseph's sons Frederick (Jonathan Frederick Braithwaite, 1883–1962) and John (John Bevan Braithwaite, 1884–1973) were admitted in 1908. In 1910 they were joined by their cousins Frank (Francis Powell Braithwaite, 1875–1952) and his brother Wilfred (R. Wilfred Braithwaite, 1877–1915), sons of the Rev. J. M. Braithwaite and brothers to Sidney, who left the partnership as they joined it. In 1912 R. H. Savory's son Rudolph (Rudolph Claude Savory, 1884–1952) came in.

The prospect in front of the newcomers was hardly reassuring. The heavy losses of 1906–1907 (p. 113 above) had been made good, after a fashion, by levies on the partners and by borrowing, but in 1910 more money was needed, evidently for repairs to the General Account. It was raised by the curious expedient of the partners forming the Highlands Syndicate to buy from the firm, by instalments covering the years from 1910 to 1913, a mixed bag of securities valued at £75,771 11s 6d. Of this sum Joseph and Cecil agreed to guarantee £42,700. There was a provision allowing the purchase price to be raised by the Syndicate from the sale of securities, but it is doubtful whether it meant very much. The transaction looks like a thin disguise for another levy on the partners' resources.[1]

In September 1911 John Braithwaite was on holiday

with his wife and his son, a baby a few months old. He was already jointly responsible, with Wilfred, 'for the general finances of the Firm, the oversight of clients' loan a/cs, the calling of balances, and the general financial arrangements.'[2] He was shocked and frightened by the firm's situation. He wrote a twelve-page letter to his father, and it survives.

First he reviewed the situation of the KCM&O as it stood in the Autumn of 1911, writing very harshly not only of Stilwell but also of Sidney and his colleagues on the London bondholders' committee, accusing Stilwell of swindling Foster & Braithwaite in the matter of the $3,000,000 Syndicate and all of them of refusing to meet obligations the details of which are lost. 'We are dealing', he wrote, 'with deliberately dishonourable men. . . . The shadow of the coming receivership looms nearer every day. . . . Such finance and such men deserve nothing else.' He begged his father to prepare a scheme for writing off the whole value of Foster & Braithwaite's investment in the KCM&O without breaking the firm.

He passed to a general review of the firm's affairs. 'We are approaching', he wrote, 'a turning point in the Firm's history. It seems to me that ever since I have had intelligent knowledge of the firm's affairs, and from things you have told me I gather it has been the same since about 1898, we have been going steadily downhill—in spite of the better results of the last two years. I entered the Firm thinking it was a strong ancient & honoured & impregnable City House. I have learnt that though we remain ancient & in a large measure honoured we are now become miserably weak & easily vulnerable.' For this lamentable state of affairs he distinguished two main reasons: 'overtrading' and company promotion, and the root of both, he implied, was the vanity of the senior partners.

'We have been overtrading,' he wrote. 'We have allowed ourselves to be drawn into schemes & commitments to a greater extent than is legitimate for a Firm with our resources.... Overtrading is nothing less than dangerous gambling.' He went on to ask how, if the firm failed, its affairs would stand investigation by a Committee of Friends. 'We should stand condemned', he concluded, 'as men who had failed culpably through indefensible speculation.' The old Quaker sanctions, it appears, still kept their force, even for a stockbroker in the year 1911.

When he turned to company promotion, his father's great speciality, he was even more severe. 'I think', he wrote, 'we have made a great mistake in regarding the bringing out of Companies as a definite branch of our Business. I believe that the time when that class of business was profitable & brought prestige has passed.... I believe we shall do very well to abandon that sort of thing.' He discussed some recent and unfortunate ventures in the promotion of oil companies, which were going through a boom brought about by the rising popularity of motor cars. 'What induced us to do it? Many causes no doubt; but partly I fear the vanity of the thought that we were Great Company Brokers—would be Pioneer Oil Brokers! Besides, we have clearly demonstrated that we are not clever enough for this work.' Blaming 'one & all collectively & without distinction', John said that the partners had been duped by 'the specious show of one Promoter after another'. Not only in this but in other ways, he said, 'an absolute paralysis of judgment seems to have overtaken us. Let us candidly acknowledge our failure to ourselves & seek to bring our minds abreast of the times & to regain an accurate & sound judgment of men & things.'

He returned at some length to the KCM&O affair as the fundamental cause of the firm's prevailing weakness and then burst out:

You may perhaps be surprised that I have spoken of the possibility of failure. It is because it has been before my mind like a nightmare day & night more or less continually for the last month & more—I have suffered it all mentally over & over again—when the hammer has gone in the House it has sounded like a knell in my ears—I have thought of the long list of our names & the awful staggering hush afterwards—in a sense the bitterness of it seems past having realized it so acutely, & anything would be a relief.[3]

This letter was never acknowledged in any way at all. Its general tone shows the strain under which John Braithwaite and, no doubt, the other partners were labouring for several years before 1914. The accounts for 1913 showed a loss on General Account of £12,635. £28,786 was 'written off KCMO', and no dividend was paid, although the rate of interest on partners' capital was put up from $4\frac{1}{2}$ per cent to 6 per cent, no doubt in compensation.[4]

When war broke out, much to everybody's surprise, in the summer of 1914, there had been no general war for 100 years. Nobody knew quite what to expect and predictions were mostly wrong. The fighting, it was generally expected, would be short, sharp, dashing and glorious— 'over by Christmas'—and the last thing most people expected was $4\frac{1}{4}$ years of siege warfare. At home there were gloomy forecasts of bad trade and heavy unemployment, but the national maxim, as stated in November 1914 by Winston Churchill, was 'business as usual' and no one foresaw the immense but lop-sided industrial expansion that 20th-century war would bring: still less, perhaps, the all-embracing Government control that would be needed to manage it.

The Stock Exchange was profoundly disturbed. As soon as the crisis in Europe became acute, towards the end of July, prices fell, Continental bourses were closed, and the foreign exchange market was disorganised. Firms suddenly found themselves with commitments that were difficult or impossible to meet, and on 29 July 1914, the day after Austria and Serbia went to war, seven firms were 'hammered'. On 31 July the Committee, faced with the possibility of ungovernable panic, closed the Stock Exchange indefinitely and put off settlements until the end of August.[5]

During the Bank Holiday week-end, 1 to 3 August, the Government over-rode the misgivings of some of its members and committed the country to war in defence of Belgian neutrality, apparently much to the satisfaction of most of the nation. As part of the process, on the Bank Holiday itself—3 August—it rushed through Parliament the Postponement of Payment Act, which held up the settlement of debts at first for one month and eventually for three. Even after that, while the war lasted and for twelve months afterwards, pressure for the repayment of loans, particularly from the banks, was in one way or another considerably eased: an uncovenanted mercy, undoubtly, for the partners in Foster & Braithwaite.[6]

The Government also prolonged the Bank Holiday by two days. When F&B's staff came back to work, on 6 August, they found awaiting them, in Joseph Braithwaite's flowing copperplate hand, slightly modified for the occasion, a notice which opened in splendidly grandiloquent terms:

In view of the supreme necessity, that every citizen of the British Empire should do his utmost to support His Majesty the King & His Government in the present time of financial and physical strain the Firm are confident that the entire Staff will be prepared to make the necessary sacrifices to attain this end.

The notice goes on to indicate what one of the sacrifices was to be:

As from the 31st inst & during the War All members of the Staff will have to submit to very substantial reductions in their salaries.

These reductions were extremely severe—salaries of £250 and £140 were halved—and they were enforced throughout the war. When men left to join the forces, however, the reductions were made good, and at Christmas 1919 £3,730 7s 6d (£3,730·37½) was paid out, in varying amounts, to 26 members of the staff, representing reductions in their pay during the years from 1914–1915 to 1918–1919. Presumably some promise of repayment had been made, but even so it is remarkable evidence of loyalty to the firm that 25 men and one woman should have waited so long to receive it.[7]

In accordance with the spirit of the day, but strikingly out of character with the Quaker background of the firm, the younger staff were urged—indeed almost commanded—to go and fight:

The National Emergency [says a notice of 3 September 1914] makes it absolutely necessary that every able bodied man under the age of 35 should immediately offer his services to his King and Country.

The firm expects that all the unmarried staff under 35 years of age will join Earl Kitchener's army at once, and also urges those who are married and eligible to take the same course.

During absence of any members of the staff on service the Firm will endeavour to do their best for their dependents and will recognise their prior claim to reinstatement.

From the partnership, Ronald Savory's son Rudolph and the brothers Frank, who had been a regular officer before he became a stockbroker, and Wilfred Braithwaite went into the Army. Savory and Frank Braithwaite survived, but Wilfred was killed at Ypres in 1915 and among the staff there were losses also.

The Stock Exchange re-opened, under various restrictions, on 4 January 1915, but prices were low and wartime business was not brisk, no doubt partly because time bargains had been forbidden. F&B's total income fell and profits vanished. As the partners put it in the minutes of their 1916 meeting, '... the War has caused a serious shrinkage in the value of securities necessitating a drastic writing down by reason of which and the contraction of business caused by the War there are no profits available for distribution.'

This minute shows how the war prolonged the problem which had faced the partners since 1911 or earlier: namely, how to get the firm out of debt and how to get rid of a burden of valueless securities arising from General Account speculation and the KCM&O collapse.

Strenuous efforts by Joseph, including three visits to New York in 1915,[8] seem to have done nothing to bring the KCM&O securities back to life, and until conditions in the stock market made profits possible again there was little to be done but follow advice given by John Braithwaite to his father in 1911. Ruin, he said then, could be averted 'by first & foremost acknowledging & facing the position ... & realizing that the remnants of our past reputation & prestige though valuable will not save us, but that hard work, *self denial*, & a cool judgment of bare facts uninfluenced by IMPRESSIONS *of men & things*, which are so apt to cloud our minds, will'.[9]

Interest was paid regularly on the partners' capital, but they received no dividends from 1913 to 1916 and they agreed to limit their drawings severely. For 1915 there was a proposal to pay allowances to such of the partners (except Joseph) as were still in the office. Cecil declined the £500 offered to him, and £1,100 was shared between John (£400), Jonathan Frederick (£400) and A. M. Barkworth (£300, reduced from £500 at his own request). For 1917 a dividend of £35 a share was paid (£646 5s (£646·25) had been paid for 1910), and for 1918, £100.

In the later years of war, then, the policy of hard work and self denial was evidently working. John Braithwaite, probably the main author of it, was by 1917 away in Italy with a Friends' Ambulance Unit, and Frederick Braithwaite was with the Friends' War Victims' Committee in Holland. It was not until 1919 that all the surviving partners were back with the firm.

The reunited partners could face the future confidently. The post-war boom and the ending of restrictions on Stock Exchange trading brought money flooding back into the market, so that F&B's total income, at £105,000 in 1919 and £108,000 in 1920, was higher than it had ever been before, and even the disastrous slump of 1920–1921 did not drag it much below £70,000, a very good figure indeed by pre-war standards. By the end of 1919 the firm's position was sound enough to write off a bad debt of £24,587 2s 6d (£24,587·12½) attributable to the International Construction Company, one of Arthur Stilwell's creations, and also to pay the partners a dividend of £350 a share. In 1920 the value of the General Account was written down by £20,408 19s 7d (£20,408·98), a dividend of £300 was paid, and it might be said that the poison of the KCM&O and other unfortunate pre-war ventures was finally out of the firm's system.[10]

Thus the firm emerged from a most dangerous crisis. As it did so, three of the senior partners—Joseph Braithwaite, R. H. Savory and A. M. Barkworth—began to clear the ground for the next generation. At the partners' annual meeting early in 1919 Joseph asked to be released from coming to the office two days a week 'as soon as John B. Braithwaite has settled back to work', and at the same meeting Cecil—who was not proposing to retire—announced the transfer of four shares to his son Geoffrey who was coming in as a partner after leaving the army. Various other share transfers were arranged, re-distributing the holdings between the generations, and at the end of 1919 R. H. Savory and A. M. Barkworth retired. Joseph himself went at the end of 1922. He had been with F&B since 1876, a partner for forty-one years, and head of the firm for thirty-four.

Cecil Braithwaite became head of the firm and remained so until he retired, in 1938. Next to him in age—some thirteen years younger—stood Col. Frank Braithwaite, and then four family partners* decisively of a younger generation: the last generation that grew to manhood before the Great War. They were Joseph's two sons Frederick and John Braithwaite, Cecil's son G. G. Braithwaite, and Rudolph Savory. Savory had wide interests in tin-mining, giving him a semi-detached viewpoint on F&B's affairs. G. G. Braithwaite, after his father retired, was transformed from the smallest shareholder into the largest (28 out of 96), but he was never disposed towards leadership. Of Col. Frank, with an aristocratic wife, a wide acquaintance and a charming disposition, much the same could be said.

Of the younger generation of partners, the most prominent was John Braithwaite. With a somewhat austere cast of mind, firmly grounded on Quaker principles, he belonged by temperament to that section of the late Victorian middle class, 'radical' in the old English sense without the revolutionary overtones which the word has lately acquired, whose monument is Hampstead Garden Suburb, where he made his home. Social conscience, solid comfort, steady purpose, all are there displayed, and also a regard for cultural and artistic interests which in John Braithwaite's case was expressed in his taste for music, photography and literature. His marriage, to Janette, daughter of Joseph Allen Baker MP (1852–1918), connected him with a family active and prominent in Liberal and, later, Labour politics. The new direction which the firm's policy took in the 1920s bore the impress of his powerful personality.

The general principles on which the firm's business was to be run—less speculative and more closely regulated than in the past—had been taking shape from 1908 onward. They were formally accepted by the partners at their annual meeting in 1915, and in 1920, when the Partnership

* A salaried partner, John Llewellyn Meade, retired in 1920. Harold Adams Wildy came in as a salaried partner in 1929 and Peter Kemp-Welch in 1936.

Deed came up for renewal, the bye-laws annexed to the new deed gave clear expression to John Braithwaite's views—he was the author of them.

The over-riding purpose in his mind, undoubtedly, was to get rid of speculative trading on General Account which offended his sense of propriety and had come close to bankrupting the firm. The new Bye-Laws included 'a general understanding that not more than £10,000 shall be invested in any one security, syndicate, or venture', and at the partners' meeting of 1921—Joseph Braithwaite's last year—matters were carried much further. 'The Firm's policy with regard to GA', Joseph recorded in the minutes, 'has been discussed and it is decided that the remaining securities on GA should be gradually liquidated and in future only Underwritings, Pools, Syndicates &c should be engaged in. This decision does not apply to the Bank shares held by the Firm or to shares in Companies to which the Firm acts as Brokers, nor does it apply to Trustee Stocks.'

This decision had the effect of concentrating the firm's attention on what the 1920 by-laws called 'the Commission side of the business', defined as 'that resulting from commissions, contangoes, interest, fees, rents and underwriting commissions': in other words, the normal business of a stockbroker, stripped of the free-wheeling speculation which had been one of the firm's major activities for two generations. The policy of liquidation seems to have been complete by 1930, and after that the volume of GA Dealings was negligible, rarely providing as much as 4 per cent of the firm's income.

The new policy was highly successful. Gross income during the '20s and '30s, from which the 'GA' element had almost disappeared, reached £157,367 in 1927 and £158,222 in 1936, figures far higher than at any time in the past. Even in the worst years—1921 (£69,623), 1924 (£73,965) and 1931 (£78,545)—income was higher than in any but half a dozen of the *best* years between the foundation of the firm and 1914. Partners' dividends varied between £200 a share in the worst years, 1921 and 1931 (when they were paid from reserves) and, in the good years, £500 (1925 and 1926), £600 (1936), £650 (1928) and £700 (1927).[11]

These results were the more remarkable for being achieved against the grain of the times. The post-war Stock Exchange showed little of the exuberant, if sometimes disreputable, vigour which had distinguished it before 1914. At the same time the British economy was already infected with the sickness from which it has not yet recovered, and that sickness arose in part, though by no means wholly, from convulsions in the world economy brought about or speeded up by the Great War.[12]

REFERENCES

1 The Highland Syndicate Limited, Agreement, 30xii10, F&B Private Papers.
2 Report of the Committee appointed to consider the allocation of duties amongst the Partners in Foster & Braithwaite 1911, Partners' Minute Book 24i11.
3 John Bevan Braithwaite to his father, 1ix11.
4 Partners' Minute Book, 4ii14.
5 Morgan and Thomas, *The Stock Exchange*, p. 217.
6 As (1), pp. 217–218.
7 'Arrears of Salary Xmas 1919', F&B Private Papers.
8 'Orient Reorganisation', F&B Private Papers.
9 As (3).
10 Partners' Minutes, Profit and Loss Accounts, 1919–1921.
11 Private Ledgers; Partners' Minutes.
12 See, for different points of view, W. Ashworth, *The International Economy*, 2nd Edn, Longmans, 1962, Chapter VII; E. J. Hobsbawm, *Industry and Empire*, Weidenfeld & Nicolson, 1968, Chapters 9 and 11; Peter Mathias, *The First Industrial Nation*, Methuen, 1969, Chapters 15, 16; David S. Landes, *The Unbound Prometheus*, CUP, 1970, Chapters 5 and 6.

Chapter VIII
The Market and the Firm
Between the Wars

Late Victorian and Edwardian Britain had enormous prestige abroad and considerable prosperity at home, widely
diffused throughout society. Prestige came from Empire:
how could a Power that ruled a quarter of the surface of
the globe be otherwise than Great? Prosperity, for many
people, came from overseas trade and overseas investment,
both linked in the public mind at home and abroad with
Imperial power, though neither, perhaps, quite so directly
dependent on it as has been imagined then and since. International trade and investment, both British and foreign,
relied on a payments system, based on gold and centred
on London, which placed no obstacles in the way of move-
ments of capital and profits.

Imposing though the British position was, there were
signs of weakness in it even before 1914. The British export
trade, though the largest in the world, was dangerously
dependent on a small group of industries. Annual average
figures from 1900 to 1909 show that 72 per cent of the
value of British exports were then coming from textiles,
iron and steel, coal, various branches of engineering, and
shipbuilding, and to this total of 72 per cent cotton textiles
alone contributed 26 per cent. What was more ominous
was that it was not in the most up-to-date branches of industry, generally speaking, that Great Britain was predominant. The British iron and steel industry, for instance,
was good at rails but hopelessly behindhand with tinplate,

and in the 20th century railway building was scarcely a growth industry, but canned goods were. In heavy electrical equipment, as in the more sophisticated branches of the chemical industry, the Germans were in the lead. British coal was exported in great quantities, but as a source of energy it was already under challenge, before 1914, by oil, and the steam engine, characteristically a British product, was giving way, on land and sea, to power plants driven by petrol, diesel fuel and electricity—itself not necessarily generated from coal.

All this suggests, and there is a great deal of other evidence pointing in the same direction, that in the export industries the general cast of mind, both among management and men, was strongly resistant to new ideas and new methods. Before 1914, partly for this reason, Great Britain was being overtaken as an industrial power not only by the United States, which had vast inherent advantages of size and natural resourses, but also by the German Empire: a circumstance not unimportant in bringing Great Britain and Germany to war with each other. When war broke out, the industrial deficiencies of Great Britain became apparent over a very wide field, including dyestuffs, drugs, certain motor components, optical goods and machine tools. Without the United States to rely on, victory would have been impossible. Moreover this very conservative attitude made it very difficult for the British export industries to adapt themselves to the drastic changes in world conditions brought about by the war.

As well as exporting goods and services, such as shipping, banking and insurance, Great Britain exported capital: an activity with which the Stock Exchange was much more closely concerned. Overseas investment, a very old-established custom, increased startlingly in the years immediately before the Great War: according to one authority, from £10 million in 1902 to £212 million in 1913, at which point it was running at a far higher rate than investment at home. For this sudden access of overseas enthusiasm investors have been much blamed, especially by the left wing, on the grounds that they were denying employment to British workers, starving the development of British industry, and building up the strength of foreign competitors.[1] It seems to be taken for granted that the export of goods was public-spirited and laudable, the export of capital selfish and despicable, and that the two were alternatives equally available.

What is less often pointed out, although W. H. Lever and others pointed it out at the time,[2] is that it was becoming increasingly difficult before 1914, and it became even more difficult later, to get British exports past tariff barriers, particularly those of the United States and the Dominions, so that the only way of gaining a foothold in many markets was by financing local manufacture: that is, by the export of capital. It is also often forgotten that a good part of the funds provided might well be laid out on plant and machinery of British manufacture, thus providing not merely profits for capitalists but employment for workers as well.

Whatever the rights and wrongs of the boom in foreign investment, the Great War destroyed it. It destroyed also many governments and other authorities which had obligations to British investors which their successors did not recognise, and it sowed the seeds of that vast and unmanageable jungle of 'reparations' and war debts which bedevilled the post-war world. In the industrial field the United States and Japan were both stronger at the end of the war than at the beginning, and the Japanese had penetrated markets for cotton textiles in India and the East which Lancashire firms had dominated for generations. Finally, the gold-based payments system of the 19th century was irreparably damaged, though the ultimate breakdown did not come until the '30s.

The prospect before Great Britain emerged in all its bleakness when the frenzied post-war boom of 1919 collapsed into the slump of 1920–1921. Unemployment shot up from about 400,000 or rather more to $2\frac{1}{2}$ million, and then settled back to a depressing row of annual figures which did not drop below 1 million until 1941 and in the worst years of the '30s—1931–1935—were permanently above 2 million and sometimes very close to 3 million.[3] The heaviest blows fell on those industries which depended most on the export trade, and for various reasons, some of which have already been suggested—Japanese competition; the replacement of coal by oil; post-war lack of demand for new ships; out-of-date products; unwillingness to reorganise—they never really recovered, so that throughout the '20s and '30s the coalfields, the shipyards and the older industrial districts generally were blighted by massive, long-lasting unemployment. The scene was not all dark. Other industries, other districts, escaped more lightly, recovered and prospered, and in general the standard of living rose. Nevertheless in the years between the wars industrial Britain suffered a severe heart attack, and the nation seemed to lack the resilience to throw off the effects, which are with us yet.

The Stock Exchange, in these circumstances, was not the rapidly growing institution that it had been during the 19th century and up to 1914. There were about 4,800 members in 1904: thirty years later, about 4,000, and the price of a nomination to membership, which in 1904 might be as high as £1,800, dwindled over thirty years to about £300.[4*] The nominal value of securities quoted, which rose during the twenty years before 1913 by 72 per cent, rose in the succeeding twenty years by only 64 per cent. In the markets chiefly representing commerce and industry in Great Britain—'Commercial and Industrial', 'Breweries and Distilleries', 'Iron and Steel'—the rate of increase, although much greater, also slowed down, from 442 per cent in the twenty pre-war years to a figure

---

* Alan Jenkins quotes a figure of £4,000 'at one point in 1927' (*The Stock Exchange Story*, p. 149), but surely this must have been highly unusual.

between 1913 and 1933—103 per cent—which can scarcely have kept up with the fall in the value of money.[5]

As a result of government borrowing during the Great War, the stock market of the '20s and '30s carried a heavy load of 'British Funds', amounting to one-third or more of the total nominal value of quoted securities, against less than 9 per cent in 1913. Foreign loans, on the other hand, were less important than before the war, partly because so many obligations had been wiped out or repudiated and partly for a reason pointed out in 1928 by a City journalist:

'The Foreign Market', [wrote A. S. J. Osborn of *The City News*], does not quite assume the importance of pre-war days when we were almost exclusively financiers to the world, a position which has become somewhat modified by American competition in the loan market during recent years.[6]

Osborn's remark is a reminder of the diminished standing of the City of London, and of Great Britain generally, in the post-war world economy, increasingly dominated by the United States.

Osborn had a poor opinion of foreign governments as borrowers, mentioning especially the perfidious French. Nevertheless he quoted a list of 58 stocks from China to Peru and taking in many other countries as well, even including Honduras. In the world of 1928 Russian Imperial stocks of 1906 and 1909 look distinctly speculative but presumably the optimist could still hope that the Bolshevists would accept czarist obligations or—better still—fall from power.

'British railways', Osborn wrote, continuing his discussion of investment possibilities, 'are not prosperous at the present time' but it was not sound, he thought, 'to regard railways as being displaced by either road transport or by the possibilities of aviation.' He hoped, as some among us are hoping yet, that all these forms of transport might in due time 'operate in unison and to ultimate economic advantage towards railway operating costs'. From the Home

Railway Market, however, that creation of Victorian capitalism in its most vigorous phase, the glory had departed.
'It now has the appearance', wrote Osborn sadly, 'of rather
tired, though not seedy, old age.'[7] Of how much else in
Great Britain of the '20s might that have been said?

Passing to the Foreign Railway Market he observed:
'what remains of the old "American Railroad Market"
really calls for no attention as the British investor parted
with the bulk of his interest in American Railroads under
forced circumstances ... during the war'. He wrote off as
'disastrous' railways in Russia, China, Mexico and Peru,
but he was enthusiastic about 'the leading railways operating in the Argentine Republic'. They were entirely, he
said, 'the conception of British enterprise' and he called
them 'probably one of the finest investments that a British
investor has ever had the opportunity of participating in
abroad'.

Railway investment overseas had a long history on the
Stock Exchange. Mining went back even further, to the
panic of 1825 and before, and was even more speculative.
It came close home to F&B through R. H. and R. C.
Savory's activities in tin, which Osborn called 'a subject
of broad speculative interest.'[8] He thought, however, that
in recent years mining had become 'such an exact science
that ... it has lost a great deal of its former speculative
appeal'. It had been overshadowed, he thought, first by
rubber in 1909–1910 and then, successively, by oil and
tobacco, 'providing great fortunes for those who purchased ambitiously at the outset and were clever enough
to take their profits before the booms had spent themselves'.

Osborn did not look on 'industrials' as suitable for the
private investor, unless he could afford to take a risk and
would watch his holdings closely. Most brokers, bank
managers, solicitors and other advisers, between the wars,
would no doubt have agreed with him, although in 1928
and 1929, under the influence of a mild boom in the British

economy and with a strong speculative wind blowing across the Atlantic, there seemed to be some ground for a rather more daring approach. Several investment trusts were formed, though since they were buying at the height of a boom which soon collapsed disastrously, the results were not happy. Unit trusts, which followed in the '30s, bought lower and did better.[9] Sir Alfred Mond (1st Lord Melchett), (1868–1930), Chairman of the newly founded ICI, believing, as he said, that 'the best answer to socialism is to make every man a capitalist', sponsored a scheme whereby ICI employees could buy ICI Ordinary shares at 2s 6d (12½p) under the mean market price, paying by instalments and receiving free shares, in proportion to their purchases, on a sliding scale linked to their rates of pay. Under this scheme 5,552 of ICI's employees became capitalists in 1928, when the shares were ranging between 29s 3d (146p) and 42s 3d (211p), and more later, some on borrowed money. Then prices began to fall, and in 1931 touched 9s 10½d (about 49p).[10]

Experience of this kind, and there was plenty of it, between 1929 and 1931 reinforced the orthodox in their view of 'industrials'. Sir Stephen Killik (1861–1938), a member of the Stock Exchange Committee, lecturing in 1934 on the work of the Stock Exchange, spoke disapprovingly of the investment trusts set up in the late '20s and austerely of the winner of an investment competition in 1928 who had gained his prize by suggesting an equal division of £1,000 between Courtaulds, Kreuger & Toll, General Motors and Woolworths. By April–May 1933, said Sir Stephen, he would have lost 80 per cent of his money, 'whilst any unimaginative layman who had invested his money in British Government stock and gone to sleep for four years would have awakened with a very handsome profit'.[11]

From the matters discussed in the last few paragraphs, it seems evident that on the Stock Exchange between the wars business was still heavily concentrated on classes of securities which had been important during the 19th century or earlier: that is to say, British and Imperial government stocks and local authority issues; foreign loans; and railway securities, British, Imperial and foreign—all of which, taken together, provided about 80 per cent of the nominal value of securities quoted on the Stock Exchange in 1933.[12] All these great 'markets' showed the effects, few of them favourable, of war, politics and the changing balance of power in the world. None held out to the investor more than bare security—many not even that—and certainly no prospect of sharing in such economic growth as the times could show.

In spite of chronic depression in British export industries; in spite of the unsettled state of world trade; in spite of the slump of 1921 and the world economic crisis of the early '30s, economic growth was considerable. The reverse face of depressed world trade and agriculture was low prices for goods which Great Britain had to import, so that the terms of trade ran in favour of British firms, leading to low prices at home and a rising standard of living for most people except the unemployed—that is, even in the very worst years of the early '30s (1931 and 1932), for somewhere between 80 per cent and 90 per cent of the population. Hence industries which relied on demand from the home market recovered very quickly from depression, when it struck, and for most of the period between the wars were expanding and developing very fast. There were about 846,000 motor vehicles, including 242,000 private cars, in Great Britain in 1921: 3 million, including nearly 2 million private cars, by 1938.[13] The BBC came into existence in 1926: 13 years later nearly every household in the country had a wireless set, and television was beginning. The middle classes might (and did) deplore the scarcity of servants, but household gadgetry was multiplying to take their place. All these industries—cars, radio, 'household durables'—required service industries to back them up, to say nothing of suppliers of components. Nor is this list of expanding industries by any means exhaustive. The British chemical industry, an indispensable supplier of materials to other industries, was firmly reorganised and made fit to compete in world markets after ICI was formed in 1926. Much the same was done for the soap, margarine and 'convenience foods' industries after Unilever was set up in 1929. There was no British canning industry at all, worth speaking of, in the '20s, but after the Metal Box Company was reorganised, largely by Sir Robert Barlow, in the early '30s, its rise was rapid.[14]

All this activity did not entirely pass the Stock Exchange by, as the official historians make clear, pointing to the formation of ICI, public issues by Morris Motors (1926 and 1935) and Ford (1928), the Electrical & Musical Industries merger of 1931, and various other large flotations. The nominal value of securities quoted in the Official List in sections of the market chiefly representing home-based companies (p. 139 above) rose from £873 million in 1913 to £1,800 million in 1939, with another £460 million in the Supplementary List, and Osborn points out that the securities of many perfectly sound companies were quoted on the provincial exchanges but did not reach the London lists at all.[15] Nevertheless we have already seen that the growth in the nominal value of securities of this class was much slower after the Great War than before. As a proportion of the total, they represented a little under 8 per cent in 1913 and twenty years later, less than 10: hardly a spectacular rise, especially in a period when some of the biggest fields of traditional Stock Exchange activity, such as foreign loans and the various railway markets, were depressed.

It is not possible to be certain of the reasons behind this rather sluggish growth, but some of them may be guessed at. In the first place, a good deal of the capital behind some of the most promising developments—cars, for instance, and 'household durables'—was not found in this country at all, but in America. More important, probably, the whole weight of tradition, as we have already observed, on the Stock Exchange and elsewhere, was against widespread investment by private individuals in industrial shares. Osborn, writing in 1928, castigated the British investor for his lack of enterprise and his ignorance—'the internal wealth of this country is enormous, but the majority of those who possess it have not been educated in the science of its adequate employment'—and he made unflattering comparisons with Americans—'in America "money talks". America is young and has arisen in a money age.'[16] He was writing on the rising market of the late '20s and he made light, by implication, of the element of risk in risk capital, especially for investors who may need to realise their holdings at inconvenient times. In the '20s and '30s, after the wartime and post-war inflation had subsided, the private investor was hardly to be blamed if he put his money where he knew he could get £1 out again, or perhaps a little more, for every £1 he put in. The big institutional investors, too, had been brought up to base their policy on an assumption of sound money, and nothing that happened in Great Britain between the wars inclined them to change their views. Industrial shares did not provide a secure home for savings, great or small.[17]

Company promotion and company finance, during the '20s and '30s, still had a questionable reputation. Some promotions and some companies were deliberately fraudulent or inherently unsound, but even where they were not, the law scarcely insisted on the disclosure of enough information to give the ordinary investor, without inside knowledge, a 'true and fair view' of propositions put in front of him. The Stock Exchange authorities, from the early '20s onward, embarked on a long and honourable course of bringing pressure to bear to make sure that greater disclosures were made than the law required before granting members permission to deal in new securities, but much of the more disreputable business went on outside the Stock Exchange and beyond their jurisdiction.

The published accounts, moreover, of companies of the highest repute did not need to reveal more than the barest minimum required to show shareholders, in the most general terms, how their capital was employed and how their profits were derived, and matters which the Directors found embarrassing or tactically sensitive could often, quite legally, be concealed. ICI was formed in a very great hurry, and as a result a higher value was set on the shares of the merging companies than their assets would justify, leading to an item of about £18 million goodwill—or 'water', as one disrespectful critic called it—being carried in the accounts from 1926 until 1956. No mention was made of it in the published version of the accounts, however, until 1941, and then it only appeared in a discreet note.[18] It was all perfectly legal, and no one questioned the honesty of the ICI Board, but what might other Boards be up to, within the law or outside it? No wonder investors were shy of 'industrials'.

This, then, was the world in which F&B were operating between the wars: a rather bewildering world in which British self-confidence had been punctured, though not yet deflated, and in which the eternal verities of the Victorian Stock Exchange, though not shattered, had been shaken; in which prudent stockbrokers still advised careful clients to invest chiefly in fixed-interest securities of carefully graded degrees of risk; in which Ordinary shares, unless the client was unusually rich, unusually daring, or unusually well-informed, were unthinkable except perhaps in carefully chosen public utilities; yet a world in which adventures with something of the old Edwardian dash and—as it turned out—even more than the Edwardian degree of risk were still possible. We must turn to the enterprises of Clarence Charles Hatry, because for a time F&B's fortunes and his were closely linked.[19]

Hatry was born in 1889 and went to school at St Paul's. By the early '20s, still young, he was well established in the City. The 16th Marquess of Winchester (1862–1962), a close associate in business and his most aristocratic victim, says: 'he was an example of the alert business brain having an unusually quick perception of any proposition, a marvellous gift for sifting the intricacies of a Balance Sheet, a power of putting his case with a clarity of expression rarely found apart from legal training, coupled with an apparent frankness which amounted to a charm of manner'.[20] Here, no doubt, lay his principal asset. As well as charming the Premier Marquess of England, he charmed other individuals who ought, perhaps, to have been rather less susceptible, including the Chairman of Lloyds Bank (Beaumont Pease) and two Braithwaites, Cecil and Frank. He also persuaded Lloyds Bank, Barclays Bank, National Provincial Bank, the Equitable Trust Company of New York, Kleinworts, and many more, to lend him considerable sums of money.[21] Among those, on the other hand, who found his charm resistible John Braithwaite seems to have been one and Montague Norman, Governor of the Bank of England, another.

At the peak of Hatry's career, between 1927 and 1929, his schemes ran wide and high. The temporary and somewhat febrile optimism of the day—a pale reflection of the boom mentality then raging through America—placed great faith in technical progress and industrial reorganisation, and was inclined to treat the provision of capital as a secondary consideration, or at any rate as a matter which great financiers like Mr Hatry (or, as it might be, Sir Alfred Mond or Sir Harry McGowan) could without difficulty attend to. Hatry mobilised an impressive array of interdependent finance companies behind department stores, behind automatic vending machinery, behind apparatus for taking automatic portrait photographs. Above all, he proposed to rationalise the entire iron and steel industry of the country, which badly needed doing.

Most of Hatry's ideas were sound, and relics of them, in quite a good state of preservation, are to be seen dotted about the industrial and commercial landscape of the

present day. The financial machinery of the country, however, would not support them, and in his efforts to make
it do so Hatry over-reached himself, abused the procedure
of the Stock Exchange, and finally broke the law. His
sudden collapse, in mid-September 1929, caused a national
sensation and something closely approaching a panic.

Foster & Braithwaite's association with Hatry did not
arise through his commercial and industrial projects, with
which they had nothing to do, but by way of his successful
assault, beginning in 1924, on the market for corporation
loans. This business, closely associated with the Consol
market, had for many years been dominated by two or
three Stock Exchange firms. Hatry set out to undercut
them, using as his vehicle a company which he formed in
1924 called Corporation & General Securities Limited, of
which the Marquess of Winchester was Chairman.[22]

Cecil Braithwaite, and probably Frank, were on chris-
tian-name terms with Winchester, whom they had known
for many years, but it does not seem to have been through
him, principally, that they became brokers to Hatry's corporation loans. The first mention of the business that Cecil
Braithwaite heard, he told Montague Norman in 1929,
was from City figures such as Sir Frank Crisp of Ashurst
Morris Crisp, solicitors; and Julian D. Marks of the Dor-
land Agency and the Staveley Trust. Cecil indicated also
that Lloyds Bank, Kleinworts and a man called Collins,
who was financial adviser to several municipal corporations, supported Hatry's campaign and F&B's part in it.
It was not widely popular on the Stock Exchange, where
it was felt that business was being diverted away from the
House, and as early as January 1925* Hatry thanked F&B
effusively and reassuringly for the help they had already

---

* This hand-written letter is dated 23 January 1924, which I assume
is a slip for 23 January 1925 because (a) Corporation & General was
not formed until 1924, (b) a loan for Plymouth, apparently Hatry's
first, was launched on 23 January 1925, making it a very suitable
occasion for a letter of thanks. W.J.R.

given him. 'This is just to let you know', he wrote, probably to Cecil, 'how very keenly I appreciate the way in which you and your partners have stood by us and helped us through our initial difficulties. . . . I am afraid that you are still worried about the possible attitude of the Banks and possibly my somewhat unusual methods. You have, I am sure nothing to worry about on either score. The banks are going to be quite impartial when they know that Collins is with us and I need hardly assure you again that I will be only too happy to follow the advice of and be guided entirely by—may I say, my friends Messrs Foster & Braithwaite.'

Between January 1925 and January 1929 F&B were associated with Corporation & General in issuing 36 loans for 30 towns. Five issued two loans and one, Wakefield, three, and as time went on they tended to borrow more at a time. The biggest loan of all was for Birmingham in October 1928: £5 million at $4\frac{1}{2}$ per cent, repayable 1948–1968, issued at $97\frac{1}{4}$. The total nominal value of the loans was £35,316,000.* Many were over-subscribed and overall only a shade over 10 per cent was left with the underwriters, although they had to take 23 per cent of the third Wakefield loan (£750,000, $4\frac{1}{2}$ per cent at 96), issued in January 1929, which may have been ominous.

F&B did not make any very large income from their share of the underwriting of these loans—a little under £19,000 in 1926, not quite £14,000 in 1927—but they valued the business, no doubt expecting growth. In June 1926 Cecil protested that after Cohen, Laming had been brought in alongside them—at the request of one of Hatry's 'valued supporters'—F&B were left with too little business to share amongst 'a most valuable list of Insurance Companies and various other friends', who would natur-

---

* The table from which these figures, and those which follow, are taken does not include the first 'Hatry' loan of all, £500,000 at $4\frac{3}{4}$ per cent for Plymouth, placed privately in January 1925 at 99.

ally say that 'now the business is successful, they are being left in the lurch.'[23]

During 1928 and 1929, as Hatry's projects grew larger and larger, he had to raise more and more money to finance them. His methods of doing so required share issues by the inter-connected companies which he controlled, intricate sleight-of-hand in transactions between them, dubious accounting practice to support—or inflate—their credit, and stage-management of share dealings—just the kind of devices, that is to say, which had long given a bad name to company finance in general and to the Stock Exchange in particular. As Hatry's conduct began to offend blatantly against the rules of fair dealing and to edge towards the confines of the law, it began also to cause F&B's partners mounting uneasiness and to harm the reputation of the firm.

In March 1928 Julian Marks, widely regarded as F&B's representative on the Board of Corporation & General, quarrelled with the other Directors over the way the profits shown in the published accounts had been arrived at, and resigned his seat. The other Directors professed great indignation at, as they said, 'an insinuation that the accounts were fraudulently or dishonestly made up', but the incident was in fact a pointer to the way things were going. The partners in F&B, instead of breaking with C&G, as Marks may have wished them to do, kept a cool neutrality, but surviving papers demonstrate their anxiety. 'Your resignation', one of the partners—probably Cecil—wrote to Marks, '. . . will not pass unnoticed, however it may be cloaked with plausible reasons. The enemies and rivals of the C&G miss nothing, and I do not need to suggest to your fertile brain the use that can and will be made of anything that can be construed as dissension on the Board.'

By the Spring of 1929 Hatry was desperately short of cash and in fact, though no one in F&B had any inkling of it, he was turning to fraud to keep his enterprises going.

He was also determined to raise £400,000 new capital for
C&G, though not with corporation loans in mind. On 24
May he told John Braithwaite what he intended to do.
'This', as Frank Braithwaite reported to Cecil, who was
fishing in the Island of Lewis, 'came as rather a jolt to John
and myself for reasons which you will readily understand.'
The principal reason was that C&G's last accounts had
shown a profit of some £80,000, 'and that this was derived
from Corporation issues is not conceivable'. It was exactly
the point on which Marks had resigned a year earlier:
Hatry was cooking the books. On top of that, the shares
had suddenly risen from 15s to 21s–21s 6d (75p to about
105p). Frank did not believe the rise was natural. Neither
he nor John wanted anything to do with the C&G issue.
Nor did C. G. Hoare of Hatry's other brokers, Cohen
Laming. All three made their views quite clear at a meeting
with Hatry and Edmund Daniels, his close associate, on 27
May, and Frank said plainly that the recent 'phenomenal'
rise was 'obviously engineered'. At this point, probably,
F&B decided to have nothing more to do with Hatry. The
decision, strongly urged by John Braithwaite, was taken
at a partners' meeting of which no record was kept.

The Wakefield loan in January 1929 seems to have been
the last for a town in the United Kingdom for which F&B
acted as C&G's brokers. By July they and Cohen Laming
were both bitterly critical of C&G's methods, especially
an announcement that the Birmingham loan of 1928 was
fully subscribed which, 'whilst theoretically correct, was
a misleading statement'. Then in the later summer of 1929
F&B and Cohen Laming were associated with an issue of
Melbourne & Metropolitan Board of Works £400,000 5
per cent Inscribed Stock 1954 which was handled by C&G
in such a way as to subject both firms of brokers to 'severe
criticism in the Stock Exchange'. On 17 September a joint
letter of protest to C&G, containing this phrase, was
drafted. It was never sent. After the Wakefield loan, C&G
handled loans for Swindon and Gloucester. At this point,

perhaps after Montague Norman had refused the Bank of England's backing for his activities in the steel industry,[24] Hatry turned to forgery to get him out of his difficulties, temporary as no doubt he hoped they would be. Fraudulent scrip in the name of C&G, allegedly exchangeable for stock of the three corporations, was printed to a value of £222,000 for the Swindon loan, £217,000 for Gloucester, £350,000 for Wakefield. This scrip, as well as genuine certificates, was used as security for widespread borrowing. Money was advanced by Cohen Laming and Lloyds Bank on good certificates: by Equitable Trust Co. of New York, Kleinworts, J. C. im Thurn & Sons, Barclays Bank, Lloyds Bank and the Porchester Trust on bad scrip, and with superb impudence Hatry persuaded some of the lenders to give up perfectly good certificates for Birmingham stock in exchange for some of his newly printed paper. As a result of all this, documents were in existence, in the summer of 1929, representing far more money than the three corporations had ever contracted to borrow. How Hatry intended to make good the difference was never made clear: perhaps he was not clear himself. It is clear, however, that the three corporations only received about half the total value of the loans and that the balance, along with the money raised on false documents, went in quite other directions.[25]

At the same time, Hatry and his associates were supporting the price of their companies' shares and raising money by bogus Stock Exchange dealings in which one Hatry company both bought and sold the shares of another—and arranged to receive an advance from the selling broker. Fraudulent documents, it was discovered later, also entered into these transactions, inflating the number of shares purporting to change hands beyond the number that really existed.[26]

That bogus dealing of some kind was going on was already apparent to Frank Braithwaite, as we have seen, by the end of May 1929. One of the jobbers involved later told an investigating sub-committee of the General Purposes Committee of the Stock Exchange that from about Christmas 1928 onward his firm, dealing chiefly in Photomaton shares, representing Hatry's venture into automatic photography, took instructions day by day from the Dundee Trust, a Hatry company, and levelled their books each evening with five specified brokers:[27] a proceeding reminiscent of C. J. Lefèvre's methods, sixty years earlier, for managing Honduras loans. At its height, this kind of dealing was widespread. The sub-committee examined 32 firms of brokers and four jobbers, and Lord Winchester thought there were 60 or more brokers buying, though only six selling.[28] During the summer of 1929, in a generally uneasy market, rumour thickened.

In September the bubble burst. On 17th and 18th the 5s (25p) shares of Photomaton patent Corporation fell from 13s 3d (about 66p) to 5s 9d (about 28p).[29] That was too much even for Hatry. He had gone to Paris on 14th, but he came quickly back again and on Thursday 19 September asked Lord Winchester to meet him at the Charing Cross Hotel. When the Marquess got there he found, in Room 80, Hatry and three of his associates, Edmund Daniels, A. E. Tabor, and J. G. G. Dixon, all men in their thirties. 'We have sent for you,' said Hatry, 'to tell you we are all criminals.' After that, they gave themselves up.[30]

Hatry's fall set off a calamitous series of bankruptcies and revealed a tangle of dealings on the Stock Exchange, some honest, some fraudulent, which took more than three months to unravel. F&B had dealings with Dundee Trust amounting to £5,581 5s (£5,851·25), including £737 10s (£737·50) on behalf of country brokers, but they became uneasy about the business early in 1929 and gave it up. What was potentially more damaging was their close association with Hatry's business in corporation loans. There was gossip in the House, and Cecil sought an interview with Montague Norman, which was granted on 4 October. Norman said he was glad Cecil had come because 'our name had been mentioned'. He listened to Cecil for an hour and asked some questions which Cecil's notes of the interview do not record in detail but which obviously he found rather embarrassing. However, Norman seemed 'quite friendly' at parting and neither the Bank nor the Committee of the Stock Exchange appear to have pursued the matter further.[31]

F&B would probably have been wise to dissociate themselves from Hatry as soon as they heard Julian Marks' opinion of C&G's 1927 accounts. The corporation loan business which they handled, however, was perfectly sound and if it was unpopular in some parts of the House that was probably only because successful competition is always unpopular with those who are successfully competed against. F&B's error, which they shared with many other individuals and firms of high reputation, was that they recognised Hatry's ability without, until too late, doubting his honesty.

Scandals on the Stock Exchange were nothing new, though the Hatry affair was a much bigger one than usual. What was new was the way the Stock Exchange authorities reacted to it.

In the past, especially in the 19th century, the Stock Exchange Committee would recognise no responsibility beyond enforcing the discipline of the Stock Exchange upon and between its own members. Beyond that they recognised no duty to the investor, either by way of guaranteeing the soundness of securities or protecting him against sharp practice. They put their views with the utmost clarity—some might say, with the utmost arrogance, great enough almost for a trade union a hundred years later—before the Parliamentary committee of the '70s (p. 86 above), and there the matter rested. The recommendations which the committees of Parliament put forward the Committee of the Stock Exchange made no pretence of carrying out.

This was an attitude which was perfectly practical at the

height of Victorian *laissez-faire* liberalism, and it was just practical right up to 1914. After the war, not so. As early as 1921 members of the Stock Exchange were forbidden to deal in new securities without the Committee's permission, and in 1934 Sir Stephen Killik, evidently speaking of a long accomplished fact, said 'dealing before allotment is absolutely prohibited.'[32] Dealings before allotment had been a constant source of scandal and complaint on the Victorian Stock Exchange, but the Committee had always refused to interfere.

The new, interventionist, attitude of the Committee emerged very strongly as soon as Hatry crashed. His central misdeed, so far as Stock Exchange dealings were concerned, related to his efforts to support shares in his companies, not to corporation loans. By issuing fraudulent documents—not share certificates, but certified transfers, transfer receipts and balance tickets—he contrived to set up transactions in more shares than really existed: a variant of the old Stock Exchange manœuvre, known as far back as the 18th century, of 'buying more than all'. The inevitable consequence, if settlement went through in the ordinary way, was alarmingly clear, not least to provincial brokers who had been heavily engaged. 'Will that mean', a provincial deputation asked in alarm, 'that people who have both good and bad shares will have to bid in the market like mad for shares they want?'[33]

That would lead to widespread chaos and ruin, within the House and outside, which the Committee were determined to prevent. Partly they sought to protect their own members, but partly also, and perhaps chiefly, they had an eye to the protection of the public: something which no Victorian Committee would ever undertake. They intended to leave no justification for anyone to say that investors had been harmed by the professional malpractice of stockbrokers. They postponed the settlement of all questionable bargains and within four days of Hatry's surrender the Chairman and Deputy Chairman of the

Committee for General Purposes, with three other members, formed themselves into a sub-committee of investigation.[33]

In January 1930 the sub-committee were able to promise settlement on 13 February. 'Its object', they said, '... is to ensure the discharge in full of all obligations to the investing public—that is to say, those ... who have sold the shares will receive payment in full, and those who have bought the shares will receive good delivery shares against payment. The scheme is designed to minimise the risk of troubles on the Stock Exchange itself, to avoid litigation ... and to facilitate the closure of this unhappy episode.'[34] The financial details, including voluntary contributions, were worked out by an unofficial 'Committee of Reference, Hatry Settlement', who closed their accounts on 13 June 1930. F&B's liability under the scheme was £2,523 5s 7d plus 'value of 5,000 Associated Automatics [shares in Associated Automatic Machine Corpn, a Hatry company]' and a voluntary contribution of £1,000, of which they received £97 16s (£97·80) back.

A settlement of this kind on the Victorian Stock Exchange would have been inconceivable, as the episodes investigated in 1875 by the Foreign Loans Committee show very clearly (Chap. V above). But the Hatry Settlement was not simply an isolated exercise in public relations or a sop to a temporarily overburdened conscience. The Committee, as we have already observed, had been moving towards a broader view of their responsibilities well before Hatry's disaster. After, they moved faster, steadily tightening rules for the protection of the public.

Soon after Hatry crashed—some have said, *because* he crashed—uneasiness set in on the New York Stock Exchange, then in the late stages of an increasingly frenzied speculative boom. Suddenly, at the end of October, uneasiness turned into panic, and over the weeks and months that followed prices plunged. General Motors common stock, to take an example, fell from $91\frac{3}{4}$ in 1929 to $7\frac{5}{8}$

in 1932. Shock waves ran throughout the world: no similar collapse was seen again for over forty years.[35]

Disaster on the New York Stock Exchange signalled the onset of the depression of the early '30s. In Great Britain the results were far less catastrophic than in USA or Germany, and in many industries, especially in the motor trade, in building and in many classes of consumer goods, recovery was rapid. Nevertheless the psychological effect was profound, probably because the 'basic industries' had been in chronic depression since 1921 and this second blow compounded their despair. For whatever reason, 'the '30s' have passed irredeemably into folklore.

On the Stock Exchange in London, in 1932, Neville Chamberlain, as Chancellor of the Exchequer, mounted an elaborate operation to convert £2,000 million War Loan from a 5 per cent rate to $3\frac{1}{2}$ per cent. Holders could have their stock redeemed at par or take the new stock with a 1 per cent cash payment, tax-free. Most of them converted, and until interest rates began to rise in the '50s they had no reason to regret doing so. In the mid '40s War Loan reached 109.

In 1937 John Braithwaite went on to the Stock Exchange Committee for General Purposes, being the third partner of his firm to serve and the first since Cecil, who was a member between 1901 and 1904. His election suggests that any damage done by Hatry to his firm's reputation, or to his own, had been repaired. He was still in control of the firm's finances and the firm, depression notwithstanding, was moderately prosperous. In 1931, the firm's worst peace-time year of the '30s, total gross income was £78,545—nearly 13 per cent higher than in 1921—and dividends of £200 a share were paid from reserves. Gross income in the best year of the '30s, 1936, was £158,222 and the rate of dividend £600 a share.

In 1938 Cecil Braithwaite retired, Frank succeeded him, and a new generation began to come into the partnership. Frederick Braithwaite's son Arthur (1911–1977) was admitted in 1938 and John Braithwaite's son David (1911–1978) in 1939, both having worked in the office for some years beforehand. They were joined in 1943 by John, son of Rudolph Savory, and after the war by M. W. Braithwaite (1948), nephew of Frank, and by C. G. Braithwaite, G. G. Braithwaite's son. G. G. Braithwaite, who had inherited his father Cecil's entire holding of 28 shares, was much the largest shareholder in the firm, although not the head of it.

REFERENCES

1 A. L. Levine, *Industrial Retardation in Britain 1880–1914*, Basic Books, New York, 1967, pp. 136–137; E. J. Hobsbawm, *Industry and Empire*, Weidenfeld & Nicolson, 1968, pp. 160–162.
2 C. H. Wilson, *History of Unilever* I, p. 99.
3 *The British Economy Key Statistics 1900–1970*, Times Newspapers Ltd, Table E.
4 Charles Duguid, *The Stock Exchange*, p. 18; Sir Stephen Killik, *The Work of the Stock Exchange*, privately printed for the Committee of the Stock Exchange, 1934, p. 23.
5 Morgan & Thomas, *The Stock Exchange*, Table V.
6 A. S. J. Osborn, *The Stock Exchange*, Broad Street Press Ltd, n.d. (1928), p. 22.
7 As (6), p. 30.
8 As (6), p. 43.
9 Killik, as (4), pp. 69, 72.
10 Reader, *ICI*, vol. 2, 63, 60, 117; (5) pp. 179–180.
11 Killik as (4), p. 74.
12 As (5), Table V.
13 Christopher I. Savage, *An Economic History of Transport*, Hutchinsons' University Library, 1959, Table II, p. 96.
14 Reader, *ICI*, vol. 2, generally; Wilson, *Unilever* vol. 2, generally; W. J. Reader, *Metal Box, a History*, Heinemann 1976, Chapters 5–7.
15 As (5), pp. 203–206, 282; as (6), p. 115.
16 As (6), p. 120.

17 W. T. C. King, *The Stock Exchange*, Allen & Unwin 1954, p. 83; Killik as (4), pp. 65–67; as (5), p. 209.
18 Reader, as (10), 8, 20.
19 On Hatry, see (5), pp. 206–208; Killik, as (14), pp. 24–27; John Vaizey, *The History of British Steel*, Weidenfeld & Nicolson, 1974, pp. 57–58; R. A. Haldane, '*With Intent to Deceive*', Blackwood, 1970, pp. 142–145, and other sources as cited.
20 16th Marquess of Winchester, *Statesmen, Financiers and Felons*, privately printed 1934, p. 250.
21 *The Times* 21i30.
22 For F&B's Hatry documents, see envelope 'Papers re Corporation Loans, Corporation & General, Securities &c' in F&B's private papers.
23 Cecil Braithwaite to C. C. Hatry, 16vi26, as (22).
24 Vaizey, as (19), p. 58.
25 As (21).
26 Stock Exchange Committee of General Purposes, Sub-Committees of a Non-Permanent Character, Investigation Sub-Committee, Guildhall MS 14609. 9 Minutes of 25x29 and generally.
27 As (26), 24ii30.
28 As (26) 27ii30; as (20), p. 267.
29 *The Economist* 28ix29, p. 562.
30 As (20), p. 269.
31 Pencil notes by Cecil Braithwaite in (22).
32 Killik as (4), p. 66.
33 As (26), p.25x29.
34 *The Times*, 13i30.
35 J. K. Galbraith, *The Great Crash 1929*, Penguin Edn 1961, pp. 113–114, Chapter VI, and generally.

Chapter IX
The Rise of the Cult of the Equity, 1939–1971

The war which broke out at the beginning of September 1939 took no one in Great Britain by surprise, and to many people of middle age and upward it seemed less like a new war than like resumed hostilities after a long armistice. The nature of the war, however, turned out very differently from the general expectation, which in a muddled way was for some kind of repeat performance of the Great War in France and the Low Countries with the added horror—very greatly feared—of aerial bombardment at home.

The Government shared in these misconceptions, and its strategic planning and predictions, so far as there were any, were wildly wrong. Administrative planning, however, which was chiefly carried out in the late '30s, was efficient, successful and very through-going. The planners, with the fairly recent experience of 1914–1918 to go on, knew that what was required was the total mobilisation of the country's resources for war. What they achieved was a centrally directed economy: a model for socialists conceived and executed under a largely conservative government.

An economy of this kind has little use for the free play of market forces. In wartime Britain they were deliberately and seriously interfered with in the interest of the supreme national objective: victory. The essential function of the Stock Exchange is to provide a free market, and in the war-time economy most of its purpose was frustrated.

Speculative dealing was checked by regulations requiring settlement in cash and forbidding continuations and options. New issues of private capital came under strict Government control. The market for large issues of Government stock was elaborately managed. Manpower disappeared along with freedom of action, for over 2,250 members and clerks went into the Services. 228—a high proportion—were killed.[1]

In the British wartime mentality the will to win was the leading motive force, but alongside it, perhaps partly in compensation for the restriction, hardship and danger which it entailed, there grew up an almost equally strong drive for radical reform of the country's society and economy. The very recent past came to be regarded with disgust and revulsion—'the '30s' were transformed almost instantaneously into folklore and legend (Malcolm Muggeridge published *The Thirties* in 1940)—and in the general atmosphere of the period it was not difficult to feel that the war was being fought as much to establish a new order in Great Britain as to overthrow one in Germany.

Political sentiment swung well to the left, and all the institutions of capitalism were suspect: not least, the Stock Exchange. There was nothing particularly new about that: what was new was that the critics of capitalism were close to power, and in 1945 they took it. The Labour Party formed a Government with a majority in the House of Commons of 146 over all other parties combined. The Stock Exchange, along with 'the private sector' generally, had an immediate problem which a new and growing industry was eager—at a price—to solve. It is no accident that the Institute of Public Relations came into being in 1948.[2]

A great deal of the idealism which had been devoted to the destruction of nazism was transferred to support of the new Government, and it set out with high hopes on the reconstruction of the British economy. That was badly needed. Recovery during the '30s had apparently gone faster in Great Britain than in the United States, but by the time war broke out deep-seated industrial weaknesses—in the steel industry, for instance, and in coal-mining—remained uncured, and six years of war made matters worse in several ways. First, radical reorganisation, already overdue, was still further postponed. Next, plant and equipment could not be renewed and modernised as they should have been. Thirdly, the underlying weakness of certain areas of British industry made for excessive dependence on the United States as the 'arsenal of democracy', with the result that in some fields, particularly at the leading edge of technical advance, British industry fell still further behind.

The Labour Government's main instrument of industrial reconstruction was nationalisation, pushed through in a torrent of ill-considered legislation between 1945 and 1951.[3] The Government's motives were chiefly political and social—to seize 'the commanding heights of the economy'—and the desire for greater business efficiency, though not absent, did not figure prominently among them. The nationalised industries were required to make a contribution to British performance in world trade at a peculiarly difficult period. They were required also to help to support an ambitious and expensive programme of 'welfare' and to realise the nation's continually stimulated demand for higher standards of living. For all these purposes sheer crude insistence on the process of creating wealth was far more necessary than the authors of the nationalisation programme were in general willing to admit.

The Bank of England, civil aviation, the coal industry, cables and wireless, transport, electricity and gas, eventually the steel industry passed successively, with greater or less controversy, into public ownership. As they did so, former owners were compensated with numerous fixed interest stocks which took their place alongside traditional gilt-edged issues, themselves much increased by war expenditure. Such a weight of Government stock, in absolute terms, had never been seen on the Stock Exchange before. It has since been maintained not only by nationalisation but by the enormous scale of borrowing which the policies of both main parties in the State require. Relatively to other classes of securities, British Government guaranteed and nationalisation stocks rose from about 35 per cent of the total nominal value of quoted securities in the mid-'30s to over 56 per cent in 1946 and then fell, over the next fifteen or twenty years, to rather under 50 per cent. No such figures had been seen, previously, since the 1860s, when the total nominal value of all quoted securities was very much lower.

This expansion of the gilt-edged market, to the world at large, was a parochial affair, not to be compared in importance with the results of the boom in industry and trade which—against most informed expectation—set in soon after the war and lasted, with minor setbacks, for a quarter of a century. In eleven of the major industrial countries of the world, including Japan, industrial production more than doubled between 1948 and 1963 and then went up by nearly half as much again by 1970. Meanwhile the value of these countries' exports of manufactures rose from $18.6 billion to nearly $155 billion. In USA the rise in production was not quite so spectacular as in Europe and Japan, but the American economy was large and vigorous enough to earn a commanding position in the world.[4]

Over a great part of the world, as a result of this boom, wealth was increasing more rapidly than ever before, and although it was distributed unequally, both as between nations and as between individuals, yet it was percolating much more widely through society than at any time in the past. At the same time as cars and television sets were becoming common in England, outboard motors were appearing on dugout canoes in Central Africa and detergent foam was floating away from dhobi ghats in India. Amid the crash of empires, there was a scramble in the successor states for something approximating to the style of life of affluent Western suburbs.

British economic growth, rather sluggish by comparison with performance elsewhere, produced a rise in the general standard of living which no one had foreseen and which seemed, in spite of a great deal of learned gloom and recurrent crises in the nation's economic affairs, to have become one of the laws of nature. In these circumstances the demand for industrial capital was brisk and the market in Ordinary shares was lively, the more so because inflation, at least for so long as Governments were committed to maintaining full employment, seemed also to have become a law of nature, so that the risk inherent in the holding of Ordinary shares (which for many years was not very great) seemed more acceptable than the certainty of loss in fixed interest securities—including the gilt-edged securities with which the market was so plentifully supplied. Even capital in redeemable securities had less purchasing power when it came out than when it went in. In irredeemable securities its fate was much worse, especially as rates of interest rose. The price of Consols, described by Charles Duguid in 1904 as 'the welfare of the world expressed in one figure',[5] fell from about 90 in 1947 to a little over 30 in 1968.[6]

This situation, in which prudence seemed to lie in what had traditionally been considered the areas of greatest risk, turned investment practice on its head. 'The cult of the equity' set in, strengthened by the Companies Act 1948, which required holding companies to publish consolidated accounts for themselves and their subsidiaries, and by investors' eagerness for capital gains, which seemed to offer protection both against high taxation and against inflation. The cult became thoroughly respectable when the law was altered in 1961 to widen the range of 'trustee securities'. For about a quarter of a century the market in Ordinary shares bowled merrily along, with prices nearly all the time on a rising trend. Memories of disasters long ago were overlaid with optimism, not to say complacency, about the present and future. 'The word "panic"', a writer on the Stock Exchange observed in the early part of 1973, 'has only appeared once in a City page headline in the past three years, and even then it wasn't justified.'[7]

The leaders of the move towards Ordinary shares were the big institutional investors, particularly the life insurance companies. Insofar as their future liabilities had to be met pound for pound, they were still in the market for fixed interest securities with appropriate dates of repayment, but increasingly, in order to keep life insurance attractive, they were looking for the kind of growth which only Ordinary shares, among Stock Exchange securities, could give. In 1946 Royal Exchange Assurance, to quote one example, had 41 per cent of the value of its total investments in British Government securities and 6 per cent in Ordinary shares, but by 1968 the position was almost exactly reversed: 35 per cent of a much larger total (£68 million against £16 million) in Ordinary shares; 8 per cent in Government securities.[8] The gilt-edged holding in 1946 was swollen by war-time pressures, but even when that is allowed for, the switch is spectacular.

Alongside the insurance companies, with investment objectives similar though not identical, were the pension funds of large businesses. These were comparatively new arrivals. Good employers since time out of mind had taken care of old employees, but usually at their own discretion, not by way of schemes conferring pension rights after retirement against contributions during employment. Moreover when such schemes were set up they were apt to be for salaried staff, not payroll workers. The ancestor of Unilever's pension fund dates from 1922, but in ICI there was no contributory scheme until 1928 and none below the level of foremen until 1937[9] and in British business generally such schemes did not proliferate until after the war. Then, especially as they began to cover the payroll as well as the staff, they began to bring very considerable funds to market, much of the money seeking a home in Ordinary shares.

This post-war surge of money into life insurance and pension contributions, alongside the luxuriant post-war growth of tax-financed welfare, has followed from the rise of a large population of wage-earners and salary-earners in stable, well-paid employment, deeply concerned with present and future security. There has been a late flowering of traditional *bourgeois* values and virtues, and allied to it, closely interlocked with life insurance, there has been a remarkable rise in house ownership—in spite of steeply rising prices—until by the mid-70s over half the house-holders in the country were said to own the houses they were living in. [10]

People of this kind, heavily and increasingly dependent on the prosperity of private capitalism, are not in general capitalists themselves, disposing of funds for direct investment through the Stock Exchange. Although more of them, as we shall see, may be in this position than is commonly supposed, yet for most, no doubt, capital is something the boss has but they haven't and investment is something to do with the football pools. They are not, that is to say, of the class from which stockbrokers' clients have traditionally been drawn, and their dependence on shareholding, though of the highest importance to them, is indirect and by many unrecognised.

One result of the 'cult of the equity' has indeed been to alter quite drastically the nature of the ownership of Ordinary shares. In the past, as we have seen in looking at Victorian and Edwardian company promotion, Ordinary shares were closely associated with the direction and management of the businesses they related to, so that even in large companies the Ordinary capital might be heavily concentrated in the hands of a few individuals or families, as for instance the first Lord Leverhulme and his son in Lever Brothers and certain Courtaulds in the business that bore their name. Public participation would normally be by way of Preference shares or perhaps Debentures. It was therefore reasonable, if not always quite accurate, to think of the Ordinary shareholder as a top-hatted, be-spatted, cigar-smoking tycoon: a vision which Sir Alfred Mond, for one, did his best to bring to life.

Large individual shareholders survive, particularly in small and medium-sized companies, but they have been overshadowed by insurance companies, pension funds, investment trusts and unit trusts. Enquiries conducted by the Department of Applied Economics at Cambridge suggest that the proportion of the Ordinary capital of 2,765 public companies, taken at market value, owned by that group of 'institutions' rose from 17.9 per cent in 1957 to 25.1 per cent in 1963 and then to 31.7 per cent in 1970. Much the biggest holders are the insurance companies—8.8 per cent in 1957, 10.0 per cent in 1963, 12.2 per cent in 1970—but by 1970 the pension funds' holdings, growing even faster, had reached 9 per cent.[11]

The investment policy of the 'institutions' has had striking effects on the ownership of large companies. Figures relating to 1973 and 1974 show about 52 per cent of the Ordinary capital of Unilever, about 47 per cent of the Ordinary capital of Burmah Oil, and about 40 per cent of the Ordinary capital of ICI in the hands of corporate shareholders.[12] Comparable figures for other large companies would probably not be very different and it is evident that at this end of the market, at least, individual shareholders, though still numerous, are quite outclassed in the size of their holdings. In Unilever in 1973, for example, the average of 79,521 individual holdings was about £172 (nominal) but the average of 757 holdings belonging to insurance companies, who between them held 18 per cent of the Ordinary capital, was £10,677.

In spite of the post-war explosion of interest in Ordinary shares, it seems doubtful whether individual shareholders represent more than a small proportion of the population of the United Kingdom: about 2.1 million people.[13]

Moreover they are inclined to be sellers rather than buyers, steadily losing ground to the institutions.

In 1957 persons, executors and trustees owned nearly 66 per cent of the Ordinary capital of the companies covered by the Cambridge enquiry already quoted. In 1963 they owned 54 per cent; in 1970, 47.4 per cent. This group of people, undoubtedly more numerous than ever before but with a declining weight in the market, represents the present state of the stockbroker's traditional customer: the private client, dealing either directly with a stockbroker or through bank managers, solicitors and other inter-mediaries.

The thirty years since the end of the 2nd World War, then, have seen very great changes in the stock market. 'British Funds', including stocks of a kind never previously seen—the stocks of the nationalised industries—have expanded enormously. As a consequence of nationalisation the Home Railway market, in which it might almost be said the Victorian Stock Exchange was born, and which for many years was the biggest market in the House, has disappeared. Foreign loans, which for thirty years or more before the Great War accounted for something like a quarter or a third of the nominal value of all quoted securi-ties, have become little more than a collection of museum pieces, sometimes profitable for the speculator. Quite against all precedent, the market in Ordinary shares has become the chief centre, apart from British Funds, of Stock Exchange activity.

Over thirty years or so, Ordinary shares have come to concern far more people than ever before. Quite how many are interested in them, directly or through life in-surance, pension funds and unit trusts, it is impossible to say, but 20 million can hardly be a high estimate, and that takes no account of dependants. All these people are heavily dependent, though no doubt few of them realise it, on the efficiency and honesty of the Stock Exchange, where the market in Ordinary shares is organised. The

Stock Exchange could at one time be regarded, without very much unfairness, as a club for professional speculators, upon whose operations outsiders intruded at their peril. Since the end of the 2nd World War the outsiders have come to include a large part of the population of the country, perhaps even a majority, and the nature of the club (for it still is a club) has altered accordingly. For ten years—1949 to 1959—of these thirty years of rapid, far-reaching change the Chairman of the Council of the Stock Exchange was John Braithwaite of the firm of Foster & Braithwaite.

The Council of the Stock Exchange, when John Braithwaite came to the Chair, was itself new, having been set up under a scheme of constitutional reform designed to get rid of the system by which the building was provided and run by proprietors, through Trustees and Managers, while the conduct of business was in the hands of members, who might or might not be proprietors, through the Committee for General Purposes. It was a cumbrous system, well-designed for acrimony, and throughout the history of the Stock Exchange as an organised institution it had been attacked periodically and from time to time reformed, notably in 1904 when measures were put in hand to make sure that all proprietors, eventually, would be members. That end had still not finally been achieved in 1945 when, after negotiations in which John Braithwaite took part, between the Trustees and Managers and the Committee for General Purposes, dual control was at last abolished and the Council of the Stock Exchange was set up. Its first form was temporary, but from 24 June 1954 its constitution was fixed to include the Government broker *ex officio* and between 30 and 36 elected members.[14]

John Braithwaite, in keeping with his temperament and his general approach to life, took the Stock Exchange very seriously. Any suggestion that it was not an institution of first-class national importance, and in particular that it was a kind of betting-shop for top people—a notion widely held and not entirely without foundation—was sure to draw his fire. 'I suppose and presume,' said Herbert Morrison in 1950, 'that the Stock Exchange has useful functions to discharge and most working people regard its work tolerantly as being rather in the same category as horse racing.' Braithwaite, whose wife was at the time campaigning on behalf of Morrison's party, delivered himself of several hundred thunderous words in reply, pointing out in particular the work done on the Stock Exchange in the field of public finance. 'Every ignorant attack upon the Stock Exchange or upon the City of London,' he concluded, 'is itself a damaging attack upon the national credit.'[15]

The Stock Exchange was an obvious target for Labour politicians, and a favourite one. In August 1951 the Chancellor of the Exchequer upset the market with a proposal for the statutory limitation of dividends. 'My friend Gaitskell's speech', said his colleague, the Minister of Local Government and Planning, '... has thrown the Stock Exchange into complete disorder and that is always good fun.' It was a flippant remark highly characteristic of the utterer, Hugh Dalton, and perhaps not of much importance, except that it came from a Minister. For this reason, no doubt, Braithwaite replied publicly in much the same tone as he had used towards Morrison.[16]

He had good grounds for feeling aggrieved. When the influential Committee on Company Law Amendment reported in 1945 they recognised that Stock Exchange rules were ahead of the law rather than abreast or, as they once might have been, entirely independent of it. They remarked on the 'searching enquiries' made before the Committee of the Stock Exchange granted permission to deal in a new security and the 'stringent requirements' which they imposed. They reported that where permission was refused or deferred, securities were practically unmarketable. They were told that between 1929 and 1939 permission had been refused twice and granted after deferment 11 times, and that in 27 cases it was still deferred.

'We recognise,' they said, 'that particularly in recent years the London Stock Exchange Committee have exercised a beneficial influence in the matter of issues' and they expressed the hope that the rules of the provincial exchanges would be brought into line with London's.[17]

Morrison and Dalton presumably knew that they were misrepresenting and undervaluing the Stock Exchange, and their utterances were important less for what they said than for the fact that, as experienced politicians, they saw fit to say it. They knew it would please their supporters and they may have felt that it would not displease some who were not normally their supporters at all. As we remarked earlier on, the institutions of private capitalism in post-war Britain had a grave problem of public relations, and the Stock Exchange more than most, because throughout its history its reputation had been much what Dalton and Morrison judged it to be when they spoke.

To this problem John Braithwaite addressed himself throughout his period as Chairman of the Stock Exchange Council. Playing down, perhaps rather too emphatically, the speculative side of the Stock Exchange's operations (which are, after all, essentially speculative in their nature), he concentrated on his conception of the Stock Exchange as part of the financial Establishment. Its central function was the organisation of the market or, as he put it, 'the efficient exchange of securities', and that, in his view, was an essential service to the community at large, not merely to some specialised, self-seeking section of it. It may be that it was in the field of public service, rather than in the business of stockbroking, that he found his own greatest satisfaction. That would certainly have been in character with the general sentiment of the Quaker circles in which he was bred and into which he married. His message, however, was not an easy one to convey to a public ignorant, sceptical, prejudiced, or for the most part apathetic.

He set out his view of the Stock Exchange's central function in his reply to Morrison:

It provides as free a market as possible for the purchase and sale of some 10,000 different securities with a total value [in 1949] exceeding £26,000 m., covering the entire field of Government, municipal and commercial finance. The Stock Exchange market is used not only by countless small investors but by Governments, nationalized boards, trade unions, co-operative societies, the public trustee, banks, insurance companies, public and private companies, and by innumerable pension funds and charitable trusts. Through the machinery of the Stock Exchange a large proportion of the nation's assets are made liquid for collection by the Government in the form of death duties or as income or surtax.... It is an essential and inseparable part of the financial machinery of the country without which neither the Government nor the commerce and industry of the nation could function efficiently. This indispensable machinery stands behind every life insurance policy, every pension, every salary and every pay packet.'[18]

A year or so later he carried even further his picture of the Stock Exchange as 'part of the financial machinery of the country'. He spoke of its 'special role, both on its own initiative and as part of the administrative machinery of company law, in ensuring that savers and investors ... have at least the maximum possible amount of clear and properly sponsored information on which to base their judgement'.[19] He was thinking, no doubt, of the pressure brought to bear on companies and company promoters, from the early 1920s onward, to provide full and honest information before their shares were dealt in on the Stock Exchange, and of the evidence given by himself and others which had helped to strengthen the 1948 Companies Act by bringing the requirements of the law more closely into line with the requirements of the Stock Exchange.

He felt very strongly about the publication of information, as well he might, for undue secretiveness has done great harm to the reputation of business in Britain. He urged the Stock Exchange itself to publish fuller statistics of its own operations. He wanted to see better, fuller and brighter company reports, backed up by brief, informal half-yearly statements. He suggested that letters announcing rights issues and allotment letters should be in language which the shareholder could understand without getting his professional advisers to translate for him.[20] Any legitimate means of making investors better informed was welcome to John Braithwaite.

This was largely because he very badly wanted to see a great growth in private, individual investment. 'If only,' he said in 1956, 'some of the hundreds of millions that are poured down the drain each year in betting on horses, dogs and football could be attracted into investment in British industry, what a fine start could be made.'[21]

Braithwaite propagated his ideas tirelessly. He made emphatic use of the opportunity offered him at the Mansion House every November and at less august gatherings, throughout the country, during the rest of the year. He pressed the Stock Exchange into actively seeking favourable publicity. This policy was an obvious defence against the hostility of the post-war Labour government, but it was not at all to the taste of the more conservatively minded members, and since the Stock Exchange is a democratic institution their powers of delay were considerable. Nevertheless in 1953 the public were admitted to the House (a measure recommended by the Royal Commission of 1877) by way of a Visitors' Gallery. A leading advertising agency—J. Walter Thompson—was retained. In 1957 the Stock Exchange formed a public relations department, and in 1958 a film was made: *My Word is my Bond*.[22] Braithwaite's fight for these novelties evidently stirred up little or no rancour against him personally, for on the day after the Visitors' Gallery opened the leader of the opposition presented him with a testimonial thanking him for it!

In the practice of the Stock Exchange itself Braithwaite

was careful of members' rights. He was chary of sharing commissions with outsiders, including the banks, and he checked at least one provincial interloper who, by quoting close prices on a narrow—and variable—range of securities and levelling his books in London each evening, competed with London, at very little risk to himself, by using the facilities which London provided. That practice he scotched, but he was not in general hostile to country brokers: indeed much the reverse. In 1939 he had been chairman of a joint conference with the provincial exchanges and in 1951 he said he would welcome the creation of a National Stock Exchange. On 25 March 1973, a few days before he died, the Federation of Stock Exchanges in Great Britain and Ireland became The Stock Exchange.[23]

Perhaps the measure by which the Chairmanship of Sir John Braithwaite—he was knighted in 1954—should chiefly be remembered is the establishment in 1950 of a Compensation Fund, designed, in effect, to insure members' clients, from the Stock Exchange's own resources, against loss arising from the default, death, dishonesty or negligence of a member. It was not a new idea—a 'guarantee fund' was being discussed in the mid-'30s, after Hatry.[24] Its importance, originally chiefly symbolic, has taken on, in times of trouble, a very practical significance.

It represents a decisive and formal acceptance by the Stock Exchange of a moral duty to the public running beyond the technical duty of organising an efficient market: an acceptance foreshadowed as far back as the 1920s and reinforced by increasingly stringent requirements for quotation, increasingly strict rules in the Stock Exchange itself, and the part played by the Stock Exchange in formulating the rules governing take-overs. It is an attitude of mind that would have astonished a Victorian stockbroker: a stockbroker, perhaps, such as Charles Branch, F&B's expert in American securities, that most uproarious of markets, who in 1876 wrote: 'The Stock Exchange is a channel, not a filter. It argues no fault in the construction of an aqueduct that the water it conveys is often dirty. The people who made the aqueduct did not supply the water, and never undertook to cleanse it.'[25]

Sir John Braithwaite, on the other hand, showed fairly clearly in his published utterances that in his opinion those who built the aqueduct should at least see that as little dirty water as possible entered it, and accept responsibility for the consequences of any that did. His vision of society, evidently, was of a property-owning democracy, with the share capital of British business widely spread among the British people: a society helped into existence and served by a Stock Exchange of high efficiency and unblemished reputation. The vision is not an ignoble one.

. . .

John Braithwaite became Chairman of the Stock Exchange Council at the age of sixty-five: an age at which most men are retiring or have retired. He held the Chairmanship for ten years, and he made it a full-time job. F&B's affairs and the business of his personal clients he attended to as best he could, often into the small hours. When he gave up the Stock Exchange Chair, in 1959, he did not retire from F&B, and indeed when his brother J. F. Braithwaite died in 1963 he was elected Head of the Firm, being then nearly eighty.

He came back to the business of stockbroking when it was altering rapidly for the reasons we have already examined: the growth of the market in Ordinary shares and the accompanying rise in the importance of the 'institutions' as stockbrokers' clients. They required service of a different kind from that which F&B, along with other old-established firms, had organised themselves for a century or more to provide for private investors.

The old-fashioned stockbroker, in giving advice on

investment, relied on native shrewdness and on information from a wide range of personal acquaintance. Of such a type were the older partners in Foster & Braithwaite: Cecil and Frank Braithwaite, for instance, and the two Savorys, Ronald and his son Rudolph. The idea of engaging staff to study economic affairs and to examine not only the published accounts but all other available material relating to companies whose securities might be of interest to investors hardly entered their heads. When it did, they scarcely took it seriously. They showed what they thought of it, in 1934, by recording in the partners' minutes a proposal to create a Statistical Department 'with a view to improving the publicity side of the business'. The traditional stockbroker, that is to say, was sceptical of the value of expert, painstaking and expensive investment analysis and did not expect to provide it, except perhaps as window-dressing, for his client. Still less did the traditional client expect to provide it for himself.

The insurance companies, the large pension funds, the unit trusts, on the other hand, employed appropriately trained staff and, as they became available, computer services for the study and analysis of everything affecting investment policy. So also did the larger merchant banks, increasingly important as advisers to companies, particularly in the take-over manœuvres of the '60s and '70s. However shrewd and experienced a stockbroker might be, he found it more and more difficult to sell his services to such alarmingly well-informed clients, or to appear to advantage as broker to a company, unless he had the support of a research department.

F&B, until late in the '60s, were to some extent cushioned against the full impact of these circumstances by the terms on which they occupied offices at 27 Austin Friars, where they had been settled since 1865 with a lease from the Drapers' Company. In 1928 the City Surveyor condemned the building as unsafe, and between 1929 and 1931 it was rebuilt at F&B's expense in return for a new

99-year lease at a rent—£1,250 a year—which, even when it was fixed, was comparatively low. After the war it soon began to look very low indeed. Sale-and-lease-back transactions with the Norwich Union, in 1954 and 1964, raised it, eventually, to £18,120, but even at that level the trend of the times was such that it was subsidising the profitability of the firm.[26]

In the early years of the 2nd World War the firm's income fell much lower than at any time in the '20s or '30s: lower, indeed, than at any time since the Great War, suggesting that the two wars, from a stockbroker's point of view, were much worse even than the worst slump, presumably partly through investors' wartime nervousness and partly through restrictions on Stock Exchange trading, particularly speculative trading. After 1945 there was a steep rise in F&B's income followed, in the late '40s, by an equally steep fall, and during the '50s income swung between £110,000 and £183,000: figures decisively, but not spectacularly, higher than between the wars. In the '60s, when the world-wide boom was at its height, income responded, ranging between £196,808 in 1966 and £333,746 two years later, with an average for the ten years 1959–1969 of £256,648.[27] This was a very much higher level of income than at any other period in the firm's history, but then no other period had brought such a sustained run of inflation.

In most years, 90 per cent or more of the firm's income arose from commission business, though occasionally, but less frequently as the years went on, business arising from new issues would contribute 10 per cent or more. The banks were still very important clients, as they had been from the beginning. They were contributing perhaps a quarter to a third of the firm's commission income,[28] but although their business was reliable it was—as ever—hardly exciting. They split commissions with the firm and the firm, by long custom, deposited a substantial 'rest' with each bank, where it earned no more than a minimal rate of interest. Moreover the banks represented the individual shareholder of the less adventurous type: scarcely the class of investor from whom, in the post-war years, the most lively business was to be expected. Nevertheless in 1962 Arthur Braithwaite was well enough satisfied with the firm's position. 'Since the last war', he wrote to his partners, 'we have made great progress, continuing the strengthening and expansion of the business, which was a feature of 1920–1939. We have now an excellent connection, and are well placed to continue our growth.'[29]

Arthur's satisfaction notwithstanding, relations between the partners were uneasy, and the uneasiness persisted from the 1930s until 1967.

It arose from disagreement between those who wished to keep the partnership on its traditional basis, as a closed shop for the descendants of Isaac Braithwaite of Kendal, and those who wished to open it to a wider range of talent, particularly as the importance of institutional investors became more and more apparent. The class of man whom the firm needed was not attracted by the offer of a salary and 'half-commission'. He wanted parity with the family partners.

The earlier phases of the conflict centred round an agreement made in 1936 with Peter Kemp-Welch. He had been at Charterhouse and at Cambridge, and he was an extremely good and versatile games player—by no means a negligible asset for a stockbroker. By the time he was thirty he had a lucrative Stock Exchange connexion, but he had disagreed with his partners and was looking for others. He was introduced to the partners in Foster & Braithwaite and they engaged him as a 'half-commission man': that is, he was to be established in Foster & Braithwaite's offices and was entitled, within specified limits, to make use of their name and goodwill. He was to split equally with them commission earned from his clients and to pay his own staff out of his own half-share. It was a common enough arrangement on the Stock Exchange.[30]

Nothing was put in writing about admitting Kemp-Welch to full partnership. It seems hardly conceivable, however, that the matter was not mentioned, whether or not any undertaking was given, the more so since a new partnership deed would be required by the time Kemp-Welch had been with the firm four years, amply long enough for all parties to get to know each other.

By 1940, when the new deed was due, it had evidently become clear to Kemp-Welch that he would never be admitted to full partnership. It must have become clear to John Braithwaite also, for each of them, in what appears to have been a concerted move, gave notice to leave the firm at the end of the war.[31] The partners accepted both resignations, thus demonstrating the strength of the conservative group, who had no intention of parting with the shares which would be required for Kemp-Welch. John Braithwaite, in the end, did not resign, but the state of feeling within the partnership may well explain his preference, from 1937 to 1959, for the affairs of the Stock Exchange rather than the business of his own firm.

Kemp-Welch duly left, in 1945, taking good institutional business with him. For twenty years after that no further attempt was made to bring in partners who were neither Braithwaites nor Savorys, though from time to time 'associates' or 'attachés' were engaged on a basis of shared commission. Of one such, in 1964, it is recorded: 'His main work would be Institutional, but we would also look to him for some statistical and research work.'[32]

In 1962, when Arthur recorded his satisfaction with the state of the firm, it stood well in the City, partly on account of Sir John Braithwaite's work as Chairman of the Stock Exchange Council, and it was prosperous enough, in good years, to pay partners dividends of £400 or even £450 a share. It stood, nevertheless, in urgent need of overhaul. This was not only a matter of bringing the nature of the business more closely into line with the development of the market. The constitution of the partnership required reconstruction. As it stood it was a beautifully preserved Victorian antique of a pattern once common but by 1962 perhaps unique in the City, for the earnings of the partners still depended entirely on the ownership of shares and bore no relation to the amount of effort the shareholders put in; nor could the partners be certain of any minimum level of earned income. In 1962, at the instance of Frederick Braithwaite and his son, Arthur, salaries for the family partners were paid for the first time, being a charge on the profits after the payment of partners' interest and before dividends. They were meant largely as an inducement to the existing partners' younger relations to come into the firm, for once more the question was beginning to arise of bringing a new generation into the partnership of F&B.[33]

Two potential partners were available: Arthur's son Jeremy (b. 1942) and Michael (b. 1943), grandson of R. C. Savory and nephew of J. N. Savory. Their family connexions were therefore unassailable, and after due apprenticeship J. N. Braithwaite became a partner in 1966 and M. B. Savory in 1967, having had 18 months' experience in the United States, where he had concentrated on investment analysis and research.

As Michael Savory came in, two partners withdrew. Their decision to do so—one was in his late '70s and the other wished to get out of stockbroking altogether—astounded some of their colleagues, but their departure, and the re-arrangement of voting power which followed, left the way clear for fundamental reorganisation of the firm and its business, both of which were overdue. The resources of the firm, both human and material, needed enlarging and modernising. Institutional business needed building up. The value of the lease of 27 Austin Friars was rising rapidly in the property boom of the late '60s and it was becoming evident that the enhanced value ought to be realised in order to protect the firm's very sound financial position against the inevitable ravages of estate duty.

Age—Sir John Braithwaite was over eighty—and ill-health among the seniors meant that much of the responsibility for reorganising the firm fell on the young, newly-joined partners. They sought new strength by merger, but after negotiations with another firm had gone as far as a public announcement the proposal was dropped, late in 1970. By that time, in parallel with the merger negotiations, the lease of 27 Austin Friars had been sold, and at the beginning of 1971 the firm moved into premises at 1 Throgmorton Avenue. From there, in 1976, they moved back into Austin Friars, this time to No. 22.

The firm also moved into a new phase of its history. On 10 February 1971 it ceased to exist in its old form. Sir John Braithwaite retired and Arthur Braithwaite became head of the firm, being succeeded two years later by his cousin, David. A new partnership was formed on 11 February 1971 on the basis of principles unheard-of in F&B's previous 146 years. The earnings of each partner are now made up partly from a fixed salary, partly from the year's dividend—if any—on the firm's capital, and partly from a sum related to the value of his work for the firm, calculated according to rules which allow for challenge by his colleagues. In the choice of new partners no restrictions are laid down, only the stipulation that they shall be admitted 'by a unanimous decision of the Partners on such terms ... as may be thought fit'.[34]

In 1968 the first full 'non-family' partner for seventy-nine years—Richard Seton Luffman—was admitted. The new deed got rid of the last traces of the Partnership Deed of 1867. It ensures that the ghostly presence of Isaac Braithwaite, which for so long haunted Austin Friars, is unlikely to walk again. It has destroyed what had become a family tyranny and yet it has preserved a family influence. The structure set up by the new deed was almost immediately tested in the worst Stock Exchange weather, perhaps, in the firm's entire history. It survived and, with it, the new model Foster & Braithwaite.

. . .

Through the windows of Foster & Braithwaite we have looked at the development of the Stock Exchange over a period of about a century and a half. The Stock Exchange too, in the mid-1970s, is in a new phase of its history: a phase arising out of a long-drawn fight to annul the results, by no means entirely undeserved, of nearly two centuries of public disapproval.

The leader of this fight, from 1949 to 1959, was Sir John Braithwaite. He was determined, and his determination was formidable, to kill the old reputation of the Stock Exchange as a club for wealthy and irresponsible gamblers and to set it alongside the Bank of England and the Treasury in the financial Establishment of the nation, having a function which would encompass responsibility for the proper conduct of all bodies and individuals concerned with the stock market.

His aim would have astonished most stockbrokers of the 19th and early 20th centuries, including probably his predecessors in the firm of Foster & Braithwaite. Many stockbrokers rather gloried in their reputation for living dangerously and saw no reason to be ashamed of an institution with its own strict, if somewhat specialised, rules of honourable behaviour. But Sir John perceived the drift of the times and his temperament urged him to go with it, carrying with him his fellow members. Among the formative influences behind many features of the Stock Exchange to-day, and behind the general spirit of its corporate policy, it is possible to detect the driving force of Sir John Braithwaite.

REFERENCES

1 Morgan & Thomas, *Stock Exchange*, pp. 228–232.
2 Geoffrey Millerson, *The Qualifying Associations*, Routledge & Kegan Paul, 1964, p. 233.
3 Sir Norman Chester, *The Nationalisation of British Industry, 1945–51*, HMSO 1975, esp. pp. 1034–1050.
4 *The British Economy Key Statistics 1900–1970*, Times Newspapers Ltd, Table N.
5 Duguid, *Stock Exchange*, p. 3.
6 As (1), Chart 1, p. 243.
7 Alan Jenkins, *The Stock Exchange Story*, Heinemann, 1973, p. 198.
8 Barry Supple, *The Royal Exchange Assurance*, CUP 1970, p. 528.
9 Wilson, *Unilever* II, p. 383; Reader, *ICI* 2, p. 69.
10 The figure accepted by the Building Societies Association is 53 per cent (1976).
11 John Moyle, *The Pattern of Ordinary Share Ownership 1957–1970*, University of Cambridge Department of Applied Economics, Occasional Paper 31, CUP 1971, Table 1, 4.
12 Annual Reports of Unilever and Burmah Oil for 1973; of ICI for 1974.
13 R.C. on the Distribution of Income and Wealth: Report No. 2. Income from Companies and its Distribution, Cmd 6172/1975, pp. 47, 105.
14 As (1), p. 232.
15 *The Times* 20ii50.
16 As (15) 1 viii 51
17 Report of the Committee on Company Law Amendment, Cmd 6659/1945, p. 14, para. 23.
18 As (15).
19 As (15), 14iii51.
20 As (15), 17xi54; 16ii56; 30iii57.
21 As (15), 16iii56.
22 As (7), p. 177; as (1), p. 238.
23 As (15), 29v51; as (7), p. 186.
24 Killik, *Work of the Stock Exchange*, p. 23.
25 Charles Branch, 'A Defence of the Stock Exchange', *Frazer's Magazine*, October 1876.

26 Partners' Minutes, 7xii28; 7ii29; 30i30; 9ii32; 18, 25viii54; 7ii55; 2vii64.
27 P&L Accounts, Partners' Minute Book, 1959–1969.
28 As (26), 6ii58, item 10.
29 As (26), 6ii62, item 6.
30 Partners' Minutes 6iv36, 25i37; Messrs Foster & Braithwaite—Mr Wildy and Mr Kemp-Welch, Agreement for a Supplemental Partnership, 30ix36, F&B Private Papers.
31 As (26), 20ii41, item 2.
32 As (26), 23x64.
33 As (26), 6ii62.
34 Partnership Agreement, 11ii72.

Appendix A
List of Partners
in Foster & Braithwaite

James Foster	1825–1855
Richard Janson	1825–1830
Isaac Braithwaite	1833–1888
Henry Waite	1846–1876
Alfred Leland Noel	1860–1888
Charles Branch	1863–1877
Alfred Braithwaite	1866–1880
Reginald Braithwaite	1873–1885
Joseph Bevan Braithwaite	1880–1922
William Huntingdon Beeman	1880–1897
Cecil Braithwaite	1886–1938
Ronald Herbert Savory	1890–1919
James Douglas Lewis	1895–1906
Alfred Montgomery Barkworth	1897–1919
Philip Isaac Beeman	1898–1915
John Sidney Braithwaite	1899–1910
John Llewellyn Mead	1908–1920
Jonathan Frederick Braithwaite	1908–1962
John Bevan Braithwaite	1908–1971
Francis Powell Braithwaite	1911–1952
Richard Wilfrid Braithwaite	1911–1915
Rudolph Claude Savory	1912–1952
Geoffrey Gawen Braithwaite	1919–1967
Harold Adams Wildy	1929–1953
Peter Wellesbourne Kemp-Welch	1936–1945
Frederick Arthur Bevan Braithwaite	1938–1972
John David Christopher Braithwaite	1939–1978
John Niedieck Savory	1943–1971

Michael Wilfred Braithwaite	1948–1971
Cecil Geoffrey Braithwaite	1949–1967
Jeremy Nils Braithwaite	1966–
Michael Berry Savory	1967–
Alfred Hubert Haslett Christmas	1968–1971
Richard Seton Luffman	1968–1976
Ian Alasdair Phillips	1971–1974
Luke Edward Timothy Hue Williams	1971–
Graeme Couper Ainsley Thom	1972–1974
Patrick Graham Hedley Hedley-Dent	1972–1974
Geoffrey Charles Morrison	1978–

Appendix B
Source Material

Foster & Braithwaite's Records

These mainly consist of Ledgers and similar books deposited in the Guildhall Library, London, which are summarised below:

Ledgers, old series, 1833–1916.
Ledgers, new series, 1917–1955.
General Account Ledgers, 1857–1929.
Partners' Account Ledgers, 1877–1900 and 1911–1918.
Sundry Accounts Ledger, 1864–1867.
Sundries Ledgers, 1889–1955.
Town Ledgers, 1896–1955.
Share Account Ledger, 1927–1949.
Journals, 1832–1845.
Subscription Books, c. 1850–c. 1908.
Clients' securities registered shares, 1910–1920.
Register of applications for new loans, 1888–1891.
Registers of applications for new issues, 1890–1896.
Account with the Bank of England, 1880–1940.
Account with National Bank, 1936–1946.

In the possession of the firm there is a series of Partners' Ledgers (distinct from Partners' Account Ledgers) from 1825 to 1959.

There is also a considerable collection of miscellaneous papers, cited in detail in the footnotes to chapters, including five volumes of 'Investment Lists' (for the benefit of clients) 1903–1914, and memoirs by Cecil Braithwaite, J. N. F. Kellas and Dudley Smith.

Published Works

Dorothy R. Adler (ed. Muriel Hidy): *British Investment in American Railways 1834–1898*, University Press of Virginia, Charlottesville, Va, 1970.

Anon: *A New Guide to the Public Funds or Every Man his own Stockbroker*, D. B. Woodward, London, n.d. (1825?).

Anon: *A Family Scene during the Panic at the Stock Exchange in May 1835*, Barker, London, 1835.

B. Braithwaite: *Banking, or Banker and Customer*, privately printed, 1900.

Keith L. Bryant Jr: *Arthur E. Stilwell, Promoter with a Hunch*, Vanderbilt University Press, Nashville, Tenn., 1971.

W. F. Crick and J. E. Wadsworth: *A Hundred Years of Banking*, Hodder & Stoughton, London, 1936.

Charles Duguid: *The Stock Exchange*, Methuen, London, 1904. *See also* W. Eden Hooper (ed.) *The Stock Exchange in the Year 1900*.

A. G. Ellinger and others: *The Post-War History of the Stock Marker 1945–1972*, Investment Research, Cambridge, 1973.

Aytoun Ellis, *Heir of Adventure*, the Story of Brown, Shipley & Co. Merchant Bankers, privately printed, n.d.

D. Morier Evans: *The Commercial Crisis 1847–1848*, David & Charles Reprints, Newton Abbot, 1969.

D. Morier Evans: *The History of the Commercial Crisis 1857–1858 and the Stock Exchange Panic of 1859*, David & Charles Reprints, Newton Abbot, 1969.

John Francis: *Chronicles and Characters of the Stock Exchange*, Longmans, London, 1855.

Roger Fulford: *Glyns 1753–1953*, Macmillan, London, 1953.

Paul Wallace Gates: *The Illinois Central Railroad and its Colonization Work*, Harvard UP, Cambridge, Mass. and Humphrey Milford, OUP, London, 1934.

George Rutledge Gibson: *The Stock Exchanges of London, Paris and New York, a Comparison*, G. P. Putnam's Sons, New York, 1889.

T. E. Gregory and A. Henderson: *The Westminster Bank through a Century*, OUP, London 1936.

Miriam Hood: *Gunboat Diplomacy 1895–1905*, Great Power Pressure in Venezuela, Allen & Unwin, London, 1975.

W. Eden Hooper (ed.): *The Stock Exchange in the Year 1900*, Spottiswoode, London, n.d. Contains 'The History of the Stock Exchange' by Charles Duguid.

F. G. Hilton-Price: *Handbook of London Bankers.* The Leadenhall Press, London, 1890–1891.

Sir Stephen H. M. Killik: *The Work of the Stock Exchange*, Committee of the Stock Exchange, London, 1934.

W. T. C. King: *The Stock Exchange*, Allen & Unwin, London, 1954.

Humphrey Lloyd: *The Quaker Lloyds in the Industrial Revolution*, Hutchinson, 1975.

Peter Mathias: *The First Industrial Nation*, Methuen, London, 1969.

E. Victor Morgan and W. A. Thomas: *The Stock Exchange Its History and Functions*, Elek Books, London, 1962.

John Moyle: *The Pattern of Ordinary Share Ownership 1957–1970*, University of Cambridge Department of Applied Economics, Occasional Paper 31, CUP, Cambridge, 1971.

R. K. Middlemas: *The Master Builders*, Hutchinson, London, 1963.

Gustavus Myers: *History of the Great American Fortunes*, Random House, New York, 1936. (First published 1907).

B. R. Mitchell and Phyllis Deane (eds.): *Abstract of British Historical Statistics*, CUP, Cambridge, 1962.

H. Osborne O'Hagan: *Leaves from my Life*, 2 vols, John Lane, The Bodley Head, London, 1929.

A. S. J. Osborn: *The Stock Exchange; its Methods and Practice*, Broad Street Press, London, n.d. (1928).

Parliamentary Papers:

Select Committee on Companies Acts 1862 and 1867, BPP 1877, VIII.

Report from the Select Committee on Loans to Foreign States; together with ... Minutes of Evidence, BPP 1875.

Report of the London Stock Exchange Commission, C2157/ 1878, HC Papers, XIX, 1878. Also Minutes of Evidence.

Report on Joint Stock Companies, C7779/1895, BPP 1895, LXXXVIII.

Francis Playford: *Practical Hints for investing Money*, Virtue, London, 6th Edn, 1869.

189

Harold Perkin: *The Age of the Railway*, Panther Books, London, 1970.

Harold Pollins: *Britain's Railways*, David & Charles, Newton Abbot, 1971.

L. S. Pressnell: *Country Banking in the Industrial Revolution*, Clarendon, Oxford, 1956.

M. C. Reed: *A History of James Capel & Co.*, privately printed 1975.

Michael Roman: *The Story of the County Company*, privately printed, n.d.

Helen P. Savory: *Memoir of Joseph Savory*, privately printed, n.d.

R. S. Sayers: *Lloyds Bank in the History of English Banking*, Clarendon, Oxford, 1957.

Francis R. Taylor: *Life of William Savory of Philadelphia 1750–1804*, Macmillan, New York, 1925.

Audrey M. Taylor: *Gilletts—Bankers at Banbury and Oxford*, Clarendon, Oxford, 1964.

A. W. Tuke and P. W. Matthews: *History of Barclays Bank*, Blades East & Blades, London, 1926.

P. G. Warren: *One Hundred Years of Stockbroking*; Heseltine Powell & Co., 1851–1951, privately printed 1951.

16th Marquess of Winchester: *Statesmen, Financiers and Felons*, privately printed 1935.

Harold Wincott: *The Stock Exchange*, Sampson Low, London, 1946.

Hartley Withers: The National Provincial Bank 1833–1933, London 1933.

I have also made use of the membership records of the Stock Exchange, and records of company prospectuses, both by courtesy of the authorities of the Stock Exchange, and I have consulted MS Minutes of the Committee for General Purposes of the Stock Exchange, including minutes of the Investigation Sub-Committee set up after the Hatry crash, all of which are deposited at the Guildhall Library London.

Lloyds Bank Limited kindly permitted me to make use of the letter books of Brown, Shipley & Co.

Index

by Dorothy L. Mackay of Duns

191